PROGRAMMING YOUR LUCID DREAMS

VON BRASCHLER

4880 Lower Valley Road, Atglen, PA 19310

Other REDFeather Titles by the Author:
Manifesting: Using Thought Forms to Visualize Real Change, ISBN 978-0-7643-6171-5
Mysterious Messages from Beyond, ISBN 978-0-7643-6286-6
Ancient Wisdom Scrolls, Past Lives, ISBN 978-0-7643-6473-0
Ancient Wisdom Scrolls, Lucid Dreams, ISBN 978-0-7643-6474-7

Other REDFeather Titles on Related Subjects:
The Esoteric Dream Book: Mastering the Magickal Symbolism of the Subconscious Mind, Dayna Winters, Patricia Gardner, and Angela Kaufman, ISBN 978-0-7643-4625-5

The Dream Gate: Understand Your Dreams, Empower Your Life, Dr. Janet Piedilato, ISBN 978-0-7643-6491-4

Copyright © 2025 by Von Braschler

Library of Congress Control Number: 2024942143

All rights reserved. No part of this work may be reproduced or used in any form or by any means—graphic, electronic, or mechanical, including photocopying or information storage and retrieval systems—without written permission from the publisher.

The scanning, uploading, and distribution of this book or any part thereof via the Internet or any other means without the permission of the publisher is illegal and punishable by law. Please purchase only authorized editions and do not participate in or encourage the electronic piracy of copyrighted materials.

"Red Feather Mind Body Spirit" logo is a trademark of Schiffer Publishing, Ltd.
"Red Feather Mind Body Spirit Feather" logo is a registered trademark of Schiffer Publishing, Ltd.

Designed by Beth Oberholtzer
Cover design by BMac
Type set in Aperto/Helvetica Now/Arno Pro

ISBN: 978-0-7643-6942-1
ePub: 978-1-5073-0559-1
Printed in China

Published by REDFeather Mind, Body, Spirit
An imprint of Schiffer Publishing, Ltd.
4880 Lower Valley Road
Atglen, PA 19310
Phone: (610) 593-1777; Fax: (610) 593-2002
Email: Info@redfeathermbs.com
Web: www.redfeathermbs.com

For our complete selection of fine books on this and related subjects, please visit our website at www.redfeathermbs.com. You may also write for a free catalog.

REDFeather Mind, Body, Spirit's titles are available at special discounts for bulk purchases for sales promotions or premiums. Special editions, including personalized covers, corporate imprints, and excerpts, can be created in large quantities for special needs. For more information, contact the publisher.

We are always looking for people to write books on new and related subjects. If you have an idea for a book, please contact us at proposals@schifferbooks.com.

Contents

Foreword by Marla Brooks, host of *Stirring the Cauldron* — 5
Introduction — 9

CHAPTER 1: When a Dream Is More Than a Dream — 13
CHAPTER 2: The Rich History of Legitimate Dreamwork — 23
CHAPTER 3: How Vivid and Real Is My Dream? — 28
CHAPTER 4: Beyond Rapid Eye Movement into Real Movement — 35
CHAPTER 5: What Can I Accomplish or Realize from My Dream? — 39
CHAPTER 6: Preparing for a Dream Journey — 46
CHAPTER 7: Establishing Perfect Body, Mind, and Spirit Harmony — 53
CHAPTER 8: Mapping Your Destination through Visualization — 60
CHAPTER 9: Step-by-Step Setup for the Dreamscape — 69
CHAPTER 10: What to Expect in the Lucid Dreamscape — 80
CHAPTER 11: Selecting Destinations Anywhere, Anytime — 86
CHAPTER 12: Confidence in Your Security and Safe Return — 94
CHAPTER 13: The Never-Ending Journey of the Hero within You — 100
CHAPTER 14: Dream Analysis and Journaling — 107
CHAPTER 15: Shared Dreams — 112
CHAPTER 16: Parallel Lives Visited in Your Dreams — 120
CHAPTER 17: Implications — 124

CHAPTER 18: Cautions and Concerns 131

CHAPTER 19: Exercises That Program Intentions, Guides,
and Shared Dreams 139

CHAPTER 20: Tips and Course Correction 149

Afterword 151
Bibliography 152
Index 157
About the Author 160

Foreword

Marla Brooks
Host of *Stirring the Cauldron*

We've been told that dreams are merely a means by which the brain processes emotions, memories, and information that have been absorbed throughout the day. Those thoughts can pop up at any time, and many remain dormant in the subconscious until they are triggered by something and then make their presence known.

This theory suggests that we have no control over our dreams and that they are just a bunch of stored memories that have a life of their own and don't mean anything because they are merely electrical brain impulses that pull random thoughts and imagery from our memories. Some people beg to differ. Freud, for example, studied dreams to understand the unconscious mind. Therefore, according to Freud, your dreams do have meaning and reveal to you your repressed wishes. Carl Jung, an early follower of Freud who broke away to develop a very different theory, claimed that the function of dreams was to compensate for those parts of the psyche that were underdeveloped in waking life. Still other dream theorists say that dreams have a problem-solving function. Dreams supposedly deal with problems we can't solve in waking life, and offer solutions.

I got to wondering if types of dreams might be a key to what the purpose of dreams might be. Some of the most common types are daydreams, recurring dreams, healing dreams, prophetic dreams, flying dreams, and nightmares. Most of those are self-explanatory, but then I read that the rarest of dreams is the lucid dream, which, simply put, is one in which you know you're dreaming while you're dreaming. In retrospect, I've had lucid dreams in the past but was unaware that they had a category all their own. I thought they were just very unusual dreams that seemed more realistic than others. I wish I had known Von Braschler back then; it would have spared me from all the head scratching and frustration in trying to figure out what that dream was all about.

My first experience of a lucid dream was years ago, when I was dreaming that I was sound asleep and suddenly woke up to find my mother and stepfather, both of whom had passed away a few years earlier, in the room. My stepdad was at the foot of my bed, and Mom was standing across the room. I was wondering why they were there, and was waiting for an explanation when my stepdad spoke up and casually asked me how I was. I thought that was an odd question, and there had to be more to their visit than that. But as soon as I told him I was fine, they were gone, and I found myself sitting up in bed, wide awake, and heard myself saying to the cat, "That was NOT a dream!"

Unlike most dreams, which escape me the minute I open my eyes, I remembered every detail of what had just transpired—from what they were wearing to my mom's uncharacteristic silence. It was a dream that was more than a dream, but it left me with a ton of unanswered questions because I had no clue as to what had occurred. Was it a ghostly visit from loved ones? Why was it so abrupt? All I could come up with was that since my mother had crossed over recently, perhaps my father was showing her how to pop back to our mundane world for a visit.

If I had only known about lucid dreams and that it was possible to plan and map our destinations to anywhere at any time, I would have immediately planned a dream journey to revisit that dream. Actually, I still can and probably will now that I've read Von's book and understand not only how lucid dreams work but how I can work with them as well. And because some lucid dreams are random and just happen, I have a couple of them on the back burner that need a bit more explanation as well.

There are exercises throughout the book to assist in the process of planning and plotting, and the journey itself; you can visit the past, the present, or the future. As Von says, "While there is a limit to how far we can see and travel in our physical world, there is literally no limit to our reach into unseen parallel universes and realities." Imagine being able to visit people, events, or places in history, and not just for fun or curiosity. These observational journeys are essential in understanding our life paths both now and throughout time. If you don't understand what you see on the first journey, you can always go back to the exact time and place and do it again without having to buy a ticket, walk through a metal detector, or fight for a window seat. You are your own trip advisor, concierge, and tour guide.

From explaining what lucid dreams are, to the how-to process, the precautions we need to be aware of, and everything in between, Von covers all bases. What I found interesting as I was reading the book was that whenever a question popped into my head, to my surprise I'd find that a few pages later, and the question was answered.

We all have moments of regret or wonder as to why certain patterns keep showing up in our lives. At times when things are going awry, I ask myself what kind of wicked person I might have been in previous lives to deserve the punishment, or karma, I'm having to go through to make up for it now. That was always a question that couldn't be answered, but now it is possible to find out.

Knowing that lucid dreams serve many purposes makes this book so special. It's possible to go back in time to watch Nero fiddle while Rome burned, revisit our own past and future lives, or even cross over to other dimensions, parallel lives, and more. Von Braschler teaches us that anything is possible to achieve, and allows us to experience the concepts that Freud, Jung, and the others were only able to dream about.

~Marla Brooks
Host of *Stirring the Cauldron* and author
of *Workplace Spells* and other books
www.marlabrooks.com

Introduction

This book on lucid dreaming will strike you as unique in at least two distinct ways. First and foremost, it will offer you step-by-step instructions in suggested exercises to help you program your own self-directed vivid dreams of insight anytime and anywhere by creatively visualizing in pictures without words. These exercises offer instructions for programming either a waking dream or an induced dream with posthypnotic prompts to guide you during sleep.

The second somewhat rare aspect of this book involves a broader scope of when and where you can travel in your lucid dreams. The guidance adapts procedures from my earlier books on time travel to give you step-by-step assistance in traveling in your dreams literally beyond normal time and space, as amazing as that might sound to you.

In my earlier books on time, *Time Shifts* and *Seven Secrets of Time Travel*, I observed how many people who experience time slips do so during lucid dreaming. Often, they are surprised to be entering the distant past in what seems like certain journey outside the body. Sometimes they are startled to travel into the future in prophetic dreams of what lies ahead. These are often unplanned lucid dreams where the spirit inside us reaches beyond our physical boundaries for the freedom of discovery. But not all such lucid dreams that involve voyages of the human consciousness beyond space-time are unplanned and surprising. I also have analyzed how many people intentionally appear to move outside normal space and time in self-programed dreams that they induce through altered states of consciousness.

As I outline in *Programming Your Lucid Dreams*, there is an ancient history of dreamwork that needs to be explored in a modern setting—an honored history of dream temples and induced dreaming. This goes back to the ancient Babylonians and Egyptians, who, thousands of years ago, understood how insightful dreams of discovery could be programmed to bring a person on a voyage of human spirit outside the physical body to discover the vast eternity of space and time.

This is something that shamans throughout the ages have understood and practiced around the world. Visionary mystics in this tradition offered themselves to their tribal community as their representative to travel far beyond the confines of their gathering to visit ancestors and find what challenges await them in the future. Some were called dream walkers, while others were called spirit walkers.

All induced a trancelike state where normal time and space seemed to fade before them, as their physical bodies became numb and their inner spirits soared far above the earth outside normal space and time.

Individual tribal members in many instances would induce personal vision quests whereby they would indulge their spirit longings for guidance in their lives. This would somewhat mirror the induced visions of tribal shamanic leaders, who would travel beyond time and space for insights to guide the entire village.

We see this successful model of induced lucid dreaming also practiced in the Far East among yoga masters. In Samadhi mysticism, which studies the wisdom yoga of consciousness or raja-yoga, young students are first taught to enter a deep dream state, where they experience travel beyond normal space and time. This dream state is intense and can last for days, wherein the spirits of students seem to travel in an energy body as pure consciousness beyond their safe confines. This exercise is thought to prepare them for greater travel of the energy body, as they develop in their awareness of latent human abilities to experience levels of reality and alternate planes of existence outside the mundane world of our physical existence.

Exercises in this new book on lucid dreaming, therefore, draw upon shamanic guides and yoga exercises in raja-yoga with new exercises for people today to explore the past and future in visionary lucid dreams. These are not guided meditations, but the framework to establish your own self-directed lucid dreams to take you outside normal time and space for discovery and personal insight. What you choose to explore is totally up to you. You can prepare your own map and establish what you want to explore, where you want to go, and what you intend to learn. Your focused intent will take you there once you have set the course and prepared yourself for the journey.

There are practical benefits to dream travel, in addition to life-altering direction, that come from exploring your ancient past and your probable future. Did you ever lose something or someone and wonder where they are? Lucid-dreaming exercises offer instantaneous reward with little discoveries that you can make by traveling outside normal time and space to find lost objects. Ever lose keys, glasses, or a wallet and wonder how to connect with them? Well, you can visualize your lost objects in your dream mapping to program exactly what you seek and what you need to know. You can go either into the past to see where you lost something, or into the future to determine when you might encounter it again in your routine daily rounds. The same rings true for finding lost pets and even people. Consider how many of our police agencies utilize the valued services of psychics, who go into a vision to determine where things might be found.

There is also a colossal upside for you in discovering vital information about your distant past or future to set you on a proper course. This course correction can help you effectively realize your own life mission. The clues from self-directed dream travel through time can help you refocus on your life path. Life mission and life path confuse most of us because we have lost our way along the long arc of our lives throughout time. This is a major concern. Our destiny and purpose in being here in this particular time involve some of those big life mysteries that confuse people most of their lifetime. Most of us deeply want to understand why we are here, what our life mission is, and how we fit into the grand picture. We wander aimlessly for decades of our lives trying to realize these answers. Connecting to our distant past and future help clarify the intended direction of our lives with purpose and grandeur.

Toward this goal, this book will explore dreams that are much more profound and informative than your normal fitful night of suppressed memories. It will outline what you can accomplish and realize from lucid dreams that are self-directed with purpose and intent. It will prepare you step by step for an actual dream journey. It will make the departure easy by establishing a new harmony of body, mind, and spirit that allows you to seamlessly leave your body in programmed dreams .

In addition, this book will give you complete mapping instructions that will build upon anything you may have heard about creative visualization. Once this mapping takes you to your targeted destination, this book will describe what you can expect. It will also give you optional settings for your dream programming, with you in control. It will position you in confident control of your security and safe return.

Moreover, you will travel the long arc of your own inner hero's journey of discovery, as you explore the guideposts and guidance that will help you complete your own life mission. This is a never-ending story of the champion inside you—your conscious spirit that longs to be free to discover, learn, grow, and achieve its primary goals along your eternal life path.

You might even discover parallel realities and universes in your dream travel, including parallel lives that you are leading, complete with people and life situations that make these realities just as real as the one you have left behind with your sleeping physical body. It is also possible that you might share a dreamscape with someone in shared dreams, where two or more people program the same destination.

You will also be provided with direction to process and internalize your dream discoveries, as only the subject and primary actor in a dreamscape can accurately hope to do. It shows how to filter your lucid dreams upon return to your waking physical body, and how to mediate on your dream encounters before recording them in a personal dream journal.

In summation, you will find here a total guide allowing you to program your own insightful lucid dreams of discovery in ways that bring you what you need to know. After all, you alone are the dreamer. These are *your* personal dreams. Only you can truly know where you want to go, who or what you want to see, and when you want to visit there.

Discover an offering of tips, cautions, concerns, and even possible course correction to guide you on your dream journey. But the trip will be totally your own, with you serving as your own travel agent, guide, and cruise director. What you will learn in advance of your dream journey are simply the steps to take in planning for your travel.

What can your dreams reveal to you? Turn the page to begin the journey.

CHAPTER 1

When a Dream Is More Than a Dream

We tend to think of dreams as superficial wandering of the restless mind, and dreamers as goofy people with their heads in the clouds. This is a generalization, of course, and not intended to describe you personally. It is simply the way that many people tend to view the common dreams that people have when they sleep at night. When we say that someone is a dreamer, that generally is not meant as a compliment to suggest a person is well grounded and focused. Even worse, a daydreamer is often seen as some sort of airhead whose mind is so unfocused that it wanders off track throughout the course of the day. No, dreamers do not have a good reputation in many circles.

These are the common dreams of a restless mind during sleep or daytime naps when we tend to drift off, of course. They come during fitful attempts to rest when the body is asleep, but the mind continues to chew on problems that you could not resolve during waking hours. Sadly, the concerns that keep us up at night about problems in our past or worries about the future sometimes cannot be forgotten by the physical brain. At such times, it simply will not shut down when the eyes are closed at night. Left to shift for itself during these downtimes, our restless brain often continues to grind away at problems without easy answers and no clues in its memory bank. Think of a calculator that is left running to chew on a problem it cannot solve, burning throughout the night until it fries its circuits and melts its frame. This happened to me once on an island in Alaska where I had rented space in an abandoned bank building for my little newspaper operation. I foolishly left an old bank calculator turned on all day and all night, until, in my absence, it started a fire that brought volunteer firefighters to put out all of the smoke.

Our typical dream during sleep is a very forgettable glimpse into submerged reflections and memories that our restless brain cannot let go, even during supposed rest time. These are not detailed dreams that offer insight or resolution, but they offer only a fading copy of memories that keep popping into our head. These are thoughts that keep flashing before us like some old movie that has special impact on us.

Psychologists often work with people with restless sleep and recurring dreams of this common variety. They say that these suppressed feelings and thoughts offer a mirror to factors that deeply move us and uncontrollably dominate our thoughts. Dream "experts" often suggest meanings behind the imagery we load into these revolving dreams of fitful nights.

Dream researchers monitor our rapid eye movement or REM sleep patterns to indicate when we are apt to have one of these recurring dream episodes during a night of intended rest. The general impression of dream researchers is that all people dream and that all of our dreams are pretty much routine and predictable as representations of things on our restless minds.

Various Kinds of Dreams

I would propose, however, that there are various kinds of dreams, with some much more profound and insightful than most people encounter in a routine night of restlessness. These are not simple dreams, but vivid encounters outside the memories of the restless mind. They have no such borders as routine dreams. Unlike common dreams, they are not based on previous recordings of information that have been stored and analyzed by the brain in its cluttered storage bank gathered in your physical life. These vivid and profound dreams, by contrast, mark the discovery of spirit or consciousness that thinks outside the box and roams in search of the unknown.

These are lucid dreams, and something far more exotic than the common dreams that most dream researchers and psychologists ponder as a mirror to our soul. Our lucid dreams are the real mirrors to the soul. They represent the free wandering of our inner spirit outside the confines of time and space.

First introduction to a lucid dream for most people seems to be a random occurrence of vivid insight. People will report having a dream that seemed much more than a dream—a journey beyond mundane reality to a realm of vivid colors, sharp images, and impactful events that unfold in a revealing manner. Such vivid dreams are often viewed as an unveiling of truth behind mystery, a parting of clouds, and profound vision of the past or glimpse into the future. People spring from their beds after such impactful dreams with clarity and enthusiasm, as though they have somehow gazed into deeper truth. If this happened during a daydream, when the body and mind were in restful repose, then the dreamer might consider the experience as divine insight or a flash of amazing understanding that somehow came to them at a moment of quiet reflection and openness.

Some people tend to daydream and find themselves miles away with a different set of people and even in another time. That cannot be simply memories played back inside your head if the people, places, and time that you experienced are not part of your physical memory bank. We might call it active, playful imagination, except that it seems too real. Also, it completely engages us to the point we appear lost in time when we return to normal consciousness. What seems to be different in the lucid dream is our heightened level of consciousness.

Then we have the case of the subconscious mind—our lower mind, which keeps drudging up problems and concerns that we try to hide. Our subconscious mind sets up its own form of random, troubling dreams. Our deep vault of stored concerns prompts recurring restless dreams as our subconscious mind releases the floodgate to our submerged memories. This is probably the brain trying to support your health and well-being by flushing out toxic thoughts. Your brain governs the routine functions of your physical body and looks after your physical survival.

In contrast, we have those dreams that would appear to engage our higher consciousness, lucid dreams that seem to take us to places we haven't really explored before and times we do not recognize as part of our physical memories.

Perhaps we should not even call these experiences dreams, except that people traditionally refer to anything that seems to happen in this way as a dream. It would appear that many of the places we go in our so-called dreams at night, when our physical bodies are asleep, would be more than simple memories or internal conjecture.

A meditation exercise can effectively set up a waking dream. I recognize that calling this a waking dream is probably an inaccurate description. It is better to think of it as a lucid dream that we experience while physically awake. Are we really dreaming during this waking dream or shifting our consciousness for visioning?

When we say that we are dreaming in the broadest sense, given the many kinds of activities we commonly call our dreams, we are using a cultural shorthand of sorts. This not only generalizes the activities involved, but also tends to minimize them as imagination that happens only inside our head, with little significance other than inward reflection. What we are saying, then, is that we were "only dreaming" and nothing more.

What about those so-called dreams where you go somewhere that you do not recognize and meet with people you do not seem to know in your waking state? Where are you? Maybe you find yourself in another time and another space, far from anything inside the room where your body resides, and outside your memory.

You might actually find yourself returning to an unusual place and time night after night, developing an ongoing relationship outside normal space-time. This is a bit like leading a double life. It would have the appearance of a parallel reality similar to the mundane world that we inhabit physically, but in an alternate time and place.

I can recall going to such a place and time for years in my lucid dreams. One of my first lucid adventures of this sort took me to a dark, rainy street corner of the town where I lived as a child. I found myself on Hewitt Avenue in Everett, Washington, in an earlier time when the buildings there looked quite different. The people there were different too. I noticed that there seemed to be no interaction of the people standing on the street in the dark rain. It was as though they all were sleepwalking and oblivious of our condition to some degree.

On one such adventure, I walked up to one of the men nearby on the street and leaned into his somewhat ethereal face. It took him a long time to acknowledge me. He seemed startled to have this sort of interaction, as though he had been staring at a still landscape.

"Do you know that you are dreaming?" I asked him.

"What? What?" he blurted. Then he disappeared in front of my eyes. The other people on the street seemed equally oblivious and dazed but remained on the street. Perhaps they were dream-walking like the man I approached and had not yet realized that they were in a real dreamscape outside normal space and time.

If this sort of alternate reality experience makes me sound insane, then I will confess that I have been insane for years. I now recognize many recurring people whom I see only in these lucid dreams, and I have an ongoing relationship with a few of them that evolves over time with each new dream sequence building on the last.

As you probably realize, simple dreams do not typically evolve or develop ongoing relationships but show us only a static situation that keeps sticking in our mind like some sort of brain clog we cannot get beyond.

A Realm Populated by Strange People

I have routinely experienced full adventures in an exotic place and time that only I seem to visit in these lucid dreams. Sometimes they are waking dreams, but most often I will set up sleeping dream conditions for myself to leave the physical world behind and visit this exotic setting. It seems just as real and fulfilling to me as the mundane world that I experience during a routine day, and maybe more.

This vivid dreamscape visited in a lucid dream is a world populated by people I do not routinely recognize from my daylight hours while not dreaming.

Indeed, this world looks different from anywhere I recall from my waking experience. I would conclude that it is not a memory or idle reflections inside my brain. And I do not think I have concocted this time and place out of pure mental imagination, since I see a reliable pattern of reality in the people and environment I see in this alternate setting.

One way to determine whether you are experiencing a lucid dream and not a simple, common dream is your perceived level of acute awareness in your dream. A high level of awareness would indicate that you are not just reprocessing memories but are actively engaged with heightened consciousness. We all have experienced enough restless dreams and nightmares to realize that a simple dream as a subconscious memory does not allow you much freedom with the static props and characters that confront you in these dreams.

You are reliving or processing old, uncomfortable memories. You try to move out of harm's way, but you are unable to move or move quickly enough. You want to control the situation but seem to have little ability. In the case of a recurring nightmare, you want a different outcome but seem to be on a rollercoaster ride without breaks or steering. It is like watching a movie and shouting for things to go a certain way, only to realize that it is only a two-dimensional recording that you are helplessly watching as an alarmed observer.

You can probably give yourself some sort of posthypnotic suggestion to cope better with these nightmares and can even try to sort out the internal problems that continue to haunt your dreams as troublesome memories. You could meditate reflectively on your nightmares and become your own best dream analyst, if you really tried. After all, nobody knows you better than you know yourself, and you should be able to interpret the symbolism and problems presented in your dreams. But that exists outside our scope here. We are looking here for dreams that are more than simple dreams of suppressed memories and suggest that some of what we commonly call dreams might be explorations into space-time shifts.

Amazing Treasures Found in Lucid Dreams

Amazing things happen from the profound insight we can collect in a lucid dream of heightened consciousness. It seems amazing and inexplicable for many people when they dream about lost people or pets and then seem to find them in their dreams. Either the lost ones find their way home shortly after these dreams or else the dreamer starts the new day with a hunch about where to start looking. We dream about what is important to us and weighs heavily on our mind, so it seems only natural for our superconsciousness to search for answers when released during peaceful repose. Our spirit cannot be denied and longs to roam for discovery. For people or pets with whom we have a deep, karmic connection, it becomes easy to see how our heightened consciousness leaps into action while our body and our brain sleeps.

Prophetic dreams would seem to be lucid, significant dreams experienced by people who look into the future. Their night visions often seem to come true in the light of day. It would appear, therefore, that they have visited the future and witnessed it for themselves. What other explanation could there be? Consider how prophets throughout time often have been called dreamers. That would appear to be close to the truth when they arise from dreams with great insight. We also must consider how such prophets are not simply forecasting the future but actually traveling into the future to bring back reports of what they have witnessed firsthand.

Many people enter a programmed dream state to find themselves in what is sometimes called soul retrieval. The idea here is that we visualize going to somewhere we feel we might have lost a key element of our essential being. Maybe it was at a time in your life when you became fragmented. Maybe it was a place far away where a part of you was taken from you, leaving you emotionally, mentally, or spiritual incomplete and empty.

It is possible to set up a meditation much like a psychologist might use in regressive therapy to return to a time and place in your life when something went wrong. Returning to that time and place will allow you to confront the problem head on, to recognize what happened to you and perhaps strengthen yourself. If you have ever gone to such a distant place in your past in a vivid dream, maybe it was not simply a memory but an actual journey. That would appear to be true, on the basis of the fact that you are not simply reliving a memory but putting yourself into a picture and seeing it more clearly with new eyes.

In a truly lucid dream that seems more than a recurring memory or nightmare, people often report a greater sense of awareness. They have a heightened sense of awareness that is different from the five physical senses that people normally use to get their bearings. The Bruce Vance books *Dreamscape* and *Mindscape* note how an active, lucid dream is often distinguished by a completely different way of seeing, hearing, smelling, touching, and tasting. In fact, he reports that the lucid dreamer's senses seem all turned upside down. Outside our regular physical world, we do not have our normal five senses but become intuitive with a new awareness that comes only with heightened consciousness of the spirit.

The first time I experienced a lucid dream, I did so accidentally. I fell back into my bed and triggered something when I struck my spine. I found myself dazed and drifting out of my physical body. It was perhaps like an accident where the spirit or consciousness instinctively evacuates the damaged body.

I mention that to suggest that you do not need to program a lucid dream for when you fall asleep. You could put your body to sleep and enter into a lucid dream without falling asleep. But programming a lucid dream and traveling outside normal time and space in a conscious body while you recline peacefully at sleep is a wonderful way to control your personal adventures into nonordinary time and space.

A meaningful lucid dream where you travel and explore in a state of heightened awareness can be set up as a waking dream or else programmed to take you on a voyage of discovery as soon as you fall asleep at night. You can program it yourself to take you wherever and whenever you want to go, with no restrictions regarding time or space.

Setting Up a Lucid Dream during Normal Sleep Time

By following a few simple steps before you fall asleep at night, you can personally program a lucid dream to take you wherever and whenever you want to go.

1. First, set up the room by making certain your area is quiet and secluded, so that you will not be interrupted and your physical body will be safe and restful.
2. Make certain that whatever you are wearing is comfortable and fits you loosely, without jewelry.
3. Ideally, there would be a little natural light that will play upon your eyes before closing them, as you recline on your back with arms and legs extended and not crossed. This allows conscious energy to flow in a clockwise fashion in your body without disruption.
4. Begin rhythmic, deep breathing. Take a full three seconds to inhale with thanksgiving, holding it inside you for a full three seconds with appreciation for the energy in it and then expelling it for three full seconds with your blessing for its future use. Continue this cycle until it begins to feel automatic.
5. Focus on the energy centers in the seven major chakras of your total body, recognizing that consciousness resides within your chakras on each of the subtle energy bodies that surround your physical self. Focus first on the red energy of the base chakra, near the bottom of your spine. Then focus on the orange energy of the spleen chakra, in the abdominal area; the yellow energy of the mental chakra, higher up; the green energy, in the heart area; the blue energy, of the brow area; the indigo area, associated with the forehead; and the violet flame,

seen above your head. Each of these chakras with their consciousness corresponds to energetic, subtle bodies and planes of existence outside the physical plane.

6. Open your eyes just a little to allow the light above you to flitter past your eyelashes. At first, you perceive only white light. Absorb and hold as much white light as you can, then increase it so that it grows in intensity.

7. Now consciously visualize the white light transforming into yellow light, building its intensity until it is bolder and brighter. Then transform the yellow light into orange light. Once you have intensified the orange light until it is bold, bright, and bouncy, transform it into red light. Once you have intensified the red from a pale red to a bold and energetic red light, transform it into a purple light. Consciously intensify the purple light from indigo to violet until it becomes a violet flame. Next, hold the full light inside you and then close your eyes.

8. Focus your conscious attention on your physical body, beginning at your toes. Consciously put your feet to sleep, allowing them to become numb and restful. Then focus on putting your legs to sleep in this way, followed by your torso, chest, arms, and head. When you have put your nose, ears, and scalp to sleep in this fashion, your physical body should be totally at rest. This will allow you to go within yourself without physical distraction.

9. Now consciously tune out all external distractions and all internal distractions. Continue until there are no thoughts or words going through your mind.

10. Next, visualize a blank screen before your mind's eye. The screen is lighted and energized, awaiting you to imprint your intentions on it.

11. On this screen, begin to visualize a picture of where and when you want to go. Draw or paint the picture without words or mental thoughts whatsoever. This picture is a design of your own making and will become your perfect road map to take you there when you are ready to leave.

12. Do not worry about the complexity of the picture that you draw. It is just a simple blueprint that you will recognize. Once you see it again, you will automatically follow it like a map that only you can read. And because it is your personal design constructed with your own consciousness, it will be an accurate map for you alone.

13. Now take in the full scope of what you have drawn, and prepare to tuck it away into the back of your mind, recognizing that when you recall it, you will follow it outside your physical body, beyond any

physical limitations of ordinary time and space, to the place and time you have selected.

14. Next, tuck it away into the back of your consciousness and prepare yourself for the journey ahead of you, giving yourself full permission to leave your body with the assurance that your physical body will be safe and rested when you leave and that you will be able to return to your physical body once you have visited your designation by simply projecting your consciousness back to your physical body.

15. If you are programming yourself for a waking dream, then you proceed directly by immediately recalling the picture you just drew to the screen in front of your mind's eye. You will automatically follow that image as an unerring personal map to the site you have determined. If you are setting up a controlled sleeping dream, then you allow yourself to drift off to sleep with the planted suggestion that you will automatically return to your designated road map when your lower conscious mind gives way during sleep mode. You fall asleep with this conscious intent. In this way, you have programmed a controlled dream outside your body.

16. When you are ready, you will automatically recall the picture to the screen in front of your mind's eye and follow the image to the place you have determined.

17. When you are there, look around to take everything in, noticing the colors and details. Look at your hands on your etheric double to recognize that you have taken a subtle energy body with you with nonphysical form.

18. Absorb what you came to study and understand. If you are visiting a prior or future version of yourself, then you might project energy to yourself there to strengthen your mental, emotional, spiritual, or causal body. That is okay. While we might hesitate to interfere with the inherent karma of another person, it is all right to relate to yourself. You will not interfere with the past but might sense the energy in your current body on many levels in a bounce-back effect.

19. All you need to do to return easily and safely to your physical body back in the meditation room is shift your conscious focus back to your physical body. This will probably happen automatically when you have explored everything that you have intended as part of a planned agenda. You will naturally snap back into your body. The entire trip outside yourself and back to the room can be instantaneous.

20. Then, when back, continue to recline on your back to quietly meditate on what you have observed. Once you have recalled the experience and

reflected on it, slowly allow physical sensation to return to your body, beginning again with your feet and working your way up your body to restore sensation. When you feel fully back in your body, gradually open your eyes and adjust yourself before attempting to sit up.

Programming a Waking Dream

As mentioned, you also can follow the above steps to set up a self-directed waking dream. The main difference is that you do not allow yourself to drift off into sleep. Consequently, you could program a lucid waking dream in the middle of the day and not wait until you are going to bed. Your launchpad could be a bed or even a mat or blanket on the floor. You could do this seated in a straight-back chair with erect posture and bare feet firmly grounded. Actually, it might work best if you recline spread-eagle on your back, with arms and legs outstretched in 45-degree angles.

This sort of waking dream where you do not actually doze off during sleep time would be similar to a meditation. People familiar with meditation could just as easily program a lucid dream by following the above steps in a meditative posture. They could enter into a lotus position, sit flat-footed and erect in a straight-back chair, or recline in the classic "dead-man pose" we described here for waking dreams, with arms and legs outstretched and positioned on the floor on your back.

CHAPTER 2
The Rich History of Legitimate Dreamwork

People interested in exploring and learning in their dreams have intentionally programmed lucid dreams of discovery for some five thousand years, dating back to the Babylonians. We know of recorded dreams as early as 3000 BCE in ancient Sumer, the city-state of the area that produced Mesopotamia, Assyria, and Babylonian civilizations. In ancient Mesopotamia, dreams were key to early divination as a source of greater truth. Kings in the Mesopotamian culture derived guidance from their dreams. Sumerian king Gudea rebuilt the Ningirsu temple sometime around 2124 BCE in the city-state of Lagash from instructions in a dream.

Gilgamesh in the Akkadian *Epic of Gilgamesh* was guided by prophetic dreams that changed the world around him. He interprets dreams as a way of looking into other worlds, and his soul traveling outside his sleeping body to visit new worlds and people beyond his world. *The Epic of Gilgamesh* describes travels to other realms and meetings with deities.

An Assyrian king built a temple to the god of dreams around 850 BCE. A later Assyrian king was visited by the goddess Ishtar, who promised him a big victory. Assyrians and Babylonians cataloged their dreams as prophecy, direction, and outlining possible scenarios to apply to their work, travel, family matters, and relationships.

Early Egyptian, Greek, and Eastern Dreamers

Egyptians as early as 2000 BCE recorded their serious dreams on papyrus leaves. The most vivid or significant dreams (what we now might call lucid dreams) were considered divine and, therefore, blessed. They believed that their dreams served as oracles with messages from their gods, and considered them as the best way to receive divine revelation.

As a result, they would take special steps to induce vivid dreams to provide them with divine direction in their lives. They would make a special trip to sanctuaries to sleep upon dream beds designed to facilitate divine encounters. These dream encounters could bring them personal comfort, divine direction, or even healing from their gods.

The ancient Greeks might be considered the first to produce a dream book: in the fifth century BCE, Antiphon wrote his book on dreams. These Greeks shared early Egyptian views on dreams as something that could be induced for guidance and divine blessing. Like the Egyptians, they felt that the soul or part of the soul left the body in exploration during dreams. They believed in Morpheus, as the god of dreams, who would visit them with useful warnings and prophecy. Dreamers who sought this divine counsel would visit temples to cultivate their dreams.

The Greek father of healing, Hippocrates, theorized that the soul received images during the day but produced images at night during dream state. Shortly after Hippocrates, Greek philosopher Aristotle (384–322 BCE) surmised that dreams could predict and even diagnose sickness.

Fellow countryman Marcus Tellius Cicero wrote in *Somnium Scipionis* that all dreams were produced by human conscious thought and resulted in visions of an insightful nature. He believed that the dreams we had were often a result of interaction we had experienced earlier in the day. That concept of dreams was shared by Greek historian Herodotus, who also believed that visions in our dreams resulted from things that concerned us during the day.

In early China, people typically believed that half of the soul was freed from the day during sleep to visit a dream realm. The other half of the soul remained securely in the physical body. In early India, dreams were simply seen as expressions of inner desires, in some cases, but also could account for the soul departing the body in divine guidance during the dream state.

Early Welsh Dreamers

Early Welsh history is highlighted by a dream narrative of visions that came to Rhonabwy, a character who visits the time of King Arthur. The early book titled *The Dream of Rhonabwy*, from the late twelfth or thirteenth century, was reincarnated in a nineteenth-century publication by Lady Charlotte Guest as *Red Book of Hergest*.

Another early Welsh dream epic is "The Dream of Macsen Wledig," a romantic tale about the Roman emperor Magnus Maximus, or Macsen Wledig in Welsh. He became, according to legend, a legionary commander in Britain from humble roots in Hispania. The commander assembled a Celtic army and then took the title of emperor of the Western Roman Empire in

383. The new emperor was defeated in battle and beheaded by the Eastern Roman emperor in 385.

Indigenous Tribes of the Americas

Native Americans actively employed vision quests as means of setting up a guided dream. Insights and prophecy from these personal vision quests would be shared with other members of the tribe upon return from this rite of passage, often preceded by prayer and fasting. Similarly, early Mexican natives believed that dreams represented a portal for contacting and visiting with ancestors. Indigenous American tribes also believed in the ability of a dream walker to induce a vision to visit ancestors as well as gods, animal spirits, and other guides. This insight would be shared with the entire tribe as meaningful advice and direction.

Early Religious and Spiritual Approaches to Dreams

Belief in the validity and significance of dreams as some sort of divine revelation dates back to the earliest religious traditions both of the East and the West, including Judaism, Christianity, Islam, Buddhism, and Hinduism. The importance of dreams is discussed in the Jewish Talmud (see 55–60 of Tractate Berachot). Early Jews apparently believed that dreams could be interpreted as insightful lessons that were applicable to daily lives and experience.

They believed that dreams came directly from the one and only true God, and, like other ancients, attempted to sort good dreams that came from God and bad dreams they believed were sent by evil spirits. They attempted to cultivate good dream experiences for divine guidance by preparing themselves to receive new divine revelations. The book of Genesis reports that Samuel, a Hebrew prophet, would prepare himself for dreaming experiences in a temple at Shiloh before the Ark of the Covenant in order to receive the word of God.

The Old Testament records early Jewish stories of prophetic dreams, many of them in Genesis. These verify a popular belief in the supernatural power in dreams. The story of Jacob's ladder was a significant dream for Jacob. In his dream, a ladder extended all the way from the earth to God in heaven above.

Early Christians, including Saint Jerome and Saint Augustine, were heavily influenced by their dreams in their lives. It was commonly believed by Catholics that God personally spoke to people in their dreams. An early Christian dream dictionary, in fact, was the *Somniale Daniels*, supposedly written by Daniel as a glossary. This glossary taught early Christians how to interpret their dreams.

The changing nature of Christianity in the Middle Ages, however, brought a more limited and dark view to dreams. The Protestant reform and the Catholic Inquisition began to see dreams differently, resurrecting beliefs in the likelihood that bad dreams could come from evil spirit. The belief then emerged that the devil himself infiltrated our dreams during sleep, attempting to deceive us. Protestant reformer Martin Luther clearly considered dreams as the handiwork of the prince of darkness, who sought to corrupt people and fill them with harmful impressions.

The Renaissance rescued dreams for Christianity in some ways, with references to traditional biblical stories of God attempting to communicate with humanity. *Joachim's Dream*, a painting by Giotto (1305), was an early fresco in the Scrovegni Chapel. A similar treatment is *Jacob's Dream*, painted by Jusepe de Ribera in 1639.

Dreams also have played an important part in the religion of Islam. This can be seen both in the history of Islam and the lives of Muslims. In fact, dreams are seen as the only way adherents can receive divine relations from God, since the death of their last great prophet, Muhammad. Consequently, Muslims consider it important to collect and reflect on these dreams in attempts to interpret their meaning.

In India, the ancient Upanishads (500–900 BCE) outline possible meanings of various dreams. One sort of dream simply explores human desires. Another sort of dream is one where the soul actually leaves the physical body and receives spiritual guidance. This early Vedic scripture describes this soul journey in dreams as an important experience of the human soul during one's lifetime.

Even today, mystic Samadhi training of novices in India involves dream training, where young initiates are taught to leave their bodies to explore and learn outside physical time and space. The yoga students are taught to consciously enter a deep dream and control their entry into these vivid out-of-body dreams of insight.

In classical Buddhism, dreams could transcend time, contain prophetic power, and be experienced by several people who share the same dream. Images of Indigenous people in Southeast Asia influenced Buddhist beliefs in the significance of dreams. In the Buddhist sacred text the *Muhavastu*, various relatives of the Buddha experienced visions of his death. In another sacred Buddhist text, the *Lalitavistara*, the future Buddha experiences specific dreams that closely resemble dreams of the previous Buddhas.

Many future Buddhas experience a similar dream about leaving home to embark on a new life. In broader Buddhist literature, dreams are often viewed as prophetic signs that indicate specific phases in the life of a character. Dream yoga is a traditional part of Buddhism that continues today.

Visionary Artists

Paintings by such visionary artists as Paul Gauguin have depicted the belief in dreams in folk spirituality in more-recent years. Gaugin's paintings of dreams and dreamers capture the earth-based spirituality of Pacific Islanders. Other artists from Goya to Rousseau, Picasso, and Salvador Dalí have been inspired by dreams and the incredible visions of dreamers.

One incredible aspect of dream art is the speculation where the dreamer's spirit goes during sleep. Dream art also explores the significance of what the dreamer actually experiences in this altered state of being.

CHAPTER 3

How Vivid and Real Is My Dream?

Before we begin to travel through time and space in the lucid dreams that we program with intent and purpose, we need to ponder how vivid and real these dreams are. This will give you confidence that you are not simply bumping around inside your restless head in a common dream of recall. It also will demonstrate how real your encounters are outside time and space when you enter a truly lucid dream, where you leave your physical body and the "here and now" far behind.

Consequently, there are two parts to this review. First, we will consider how vivid the dream is that you enter, to determine whether you've entered a dreamscape outside normal time and space or simply wandered into your restless mind of worries and concerns that will not sleep after your head hits the pillow. Such idle wandering without purpose in a common dream can happen to you just as easily during daylight hours, of course, in a so-called daydream. We often overlook our daydreams as throwaway visions or flights of the imagination, but we should try to control our dreams to make them meaningful.

Let us recognize from the outset, then, that a common, uncontrolled dream that simply comes to us as a result of the restless mind is seldom really vivid like a lucid dream. Such common dreams rarely have a focus that allows you to examine the concerns that spill over from past problems or your anticipation of events before you. These are worry dreams without definition and will probably give you little insight into problems or concerns that vex you—even as you try to rest—because the physical brain that has recycled them could not resolve them even when fully activated when you were awake and physically alert.

In such common, meaningless dreams, you will find yourself reliving past events or conflicts. You might be actively involved as a character, but really as an actor in a prescripted play that you are reenacting. There is no applause, since you are the only actor, playing all the parts or acting against shadow representations. There might appear to be symbolism in your dream, but only insofar as your physical mind tries to put a bow on the situation to tie it all together for you once and for all. Always keep in mind, however, that these are the ramblings of a disturbed mind that is grasping for answers it cannot easily find. As a result, there is little meaningful resolution or insight in any such common dream. In fact, they tend to appear as nightmares. Even the happy memories in such recollections during sleep are unfulfilling, since they do not offer insight or resolution.

The proof that these common dreams are simply recycled memories without programming or focus is evident in the pattern of the simple dreams. Is this a dream that you have over and over again, in much the same way or with slight variation? Does it always end pretty much the same way, without resolution or insight? Does such a dream—repeated with slight variations—leave you restless in the end? That is because such simple dreams resemble little train wrecks as problem scenarios stored inside your physical brain's memory banks. They slip out when the body is resting and the mind is placed into a restful repose where it can idle about. The physical brain refuses to go to sleep fully and to cease processing previously stored information until you put it to full stop. This book seeks to show you how to put your physical brain to rest to allow your higher consciousness to assume direction.

We cannot bestow glorious tribute to a physical brain beyond what it is primarily intended to do for us. Our brain is like the engine that runs your physical body, telling the heart to pump, the lungs to breathe, the legs to move, and injuries to self-correct, in the magnificent anatomy and physiology that is our human physical body. It does a magnificent job in most respects but cannot be expected to resolve problems it cannot solve when fully awake. We cannot ask it to reach beyond time and space into what it considers the vast unknown. It knows only what information has been stored in its memory to try to process thoughtfully in sound analysis in the here and now. Our physical brain is like a simple, little computer with limited scope and function. You might think of it like some sort of a pocket calculator. There are some places it cannot function well. It cannot go beyond the limits of what information has been previously stored in it for processing and analysis. It cannot reach beyond immediate space and time.

For that, you need a supercomputer. You need a computer that can think for itself and exceed its initial programming. You need heightened consciousness, intelligent energy that exists within you and outside you on all levels as your connection to all of life and all of creation. This is the sort of electromagnetic energy that drives and sustains all of life, from the greatest galaxy to the smallest atom, with us in the middle of it all.

No, the dreams that our restless mind resurrects when we enter routine dream state in an unprogrammed dreamscape without intent or direction are not really vivid. They present us with a dim world of shadowy figures and representational events and characters that continue to grind away inside our heads unless turned off. This view is not meant as a criticism or slight of your physical mind or that of anyone. It is just an honest view of the role of our physical brain, which we often extol for all that we program into it and get out of it. It performs up to its task very well, often continuing to function for us long after vital organs have ceased to serve us in our physical bodies. It is like a ship's captain who is always vigilant and even willing to go down with the ship.

In hopes that our analytical brains continue to resolve our innermost problems, however, we often hop out of bed in the morning to jot down our impressions of recurring shadow images from our common dreams in dream journals, to ponder the symbolism and meaning of these dreams. We cannot confuse these restless wanderings of a sleepless mind, though, with vivid memories of a lucid dream.

Vivid Images in a Lucid Dream

The lucid dream, filled with insight, discovery, and meaning, will appear much more vivid in many ways. It is much more than a simple, common dream that comes to us in a restless night when our physical mind cannot fully rest. So, you must ask yourself when you enter such a vivid and colorful dream outside normal restless dream wandering whether you have entered a lucid dream. Many people occasionally enter into such lucid dreams without advance planning. Consequently, it is important to orient yourself in these dreams to determine the possibilities. There are few possibilities, as we have seen, in a routine dream triggered by a restless mind. But the sky becomes the limit during a lucid dream.

Orient yourself if you are conscious that you are dreaming, to determine whether you have acute awareness and mobility. Look at the backs of your hands, which likely will appear as etheric energy forms. See how easily you can move about. Notice how bright and abundant the colors are in your dream. If your dream is colorful, then you have advanced beyond the simple shadow world of black and gray in restless dreams and entered into a totally new dreamscape.

You will become acutely aware of greater detail in a lucid dream. The characters and entire scene will appear sharper. You have replaced your normal physical perceptive skills in this state of heightened consciousness with innate awareness. Gone are your physical eyes, ears, and sense of touch. In their place, you have new ears, new eyes, and a keen sense of touch.

As a result, things will appear to you as more vivid, with greater color and definition. Your heightened consciousness, as energized intelligence, gives you the ability to see things more clearly in this state. In a sense, you can see through the superficial surface impression of people and things and appreciate what is beneath the surface. This is how we begin to comprehend purpose, intent, and the causal nature of energetic bodies that normally appear to us simply as physical matter that reflects light.

This lucid dreamscape is alive and vibrant, while routine dreams of a restless mind are simply shadows of things we have stored in our physical memory. As midwestern cowboy poet Bruce Vance outlined in his stunning dream books, you are likely to discover colors, smells, and other impressions normally filtered through your physical sense as vastly different in a new realm of discovery that is more colorful, sharply defined, and impressive to behold.

You have gone beyond the normal physical realm you know, with normal physical gifts of perception that commonly filter what you observe as reality. Now you are seeing with acute, new awareness into the real intent behind surface appearances, with a focus that is foreign to your physical experiences. There is nothing in your memory banks as a frame of reference to orient you here. This is an open field of a running bold spirit that has been freed from your physical body.

As you enter this new reality, you are driven by emotional energy, mental energy, and causal energy that have been activated and directed by the consciousness that resides on all subtle energy bodies that make us whole. Most people, sadly, recognize only their dense, physical body. This overlooks the luminous egg, as Carlos Castaneda colorfully described our outer energy bodies in his novels of supernatural discovery. It overlooks the model outlined by Eastern spiritual science, which shows a layering of subtle bodies that surround our physical body as energy that connects us to the mental plane of existence, the emotional plane, the causal plane, and higher spiritual planes of reality.

The dream traveler who enters a lucid dream—whether intentionally or unintentionally—will journey beyond the physical surroundings of the dreamer to realms outside normal time and space with these energy bodies. The energy bodies connect us to other planes of existence, as described by the role they play within our holistic health from emotional, mental, causal, or higher spiritual aspects of our lives. Sadly, again, many people never recognize or explore these higher spiritual aspects or the planes of existence outside their physical nature.

With these subtle energy bodies, driven by our higher consciousness, a dreamer in a so-called lucid dream can go virtually anywhere and to any time, experiencing other realities with agility. The lucid dreamer can fly, bilocate in a flash, create with a thought, and do virtually anything. In fact, it is challenging to imagine anything that a lucid dreamer could not do or discover by traveling in these energy bodies in heightened consciousness.

We must recognize that the physical body of the dreamer is safely resting, while the conscious bodies of the dreamer roam far and wide. This is, after all, a journey of discovery of personal interest to the dreamer. The dreamer can travel broadly between the worlds. And when a person consciously programs a personal lucid dream, the dream can be directed to reach a specific place and time to events and situations that are preprogrammed. In this manner, the lucid dream in all its vividness can be drawn like a map by the dreamer with focused intent. The dreamer begins with focused intent in setting up the dream and enjoys focused intent throughout the dream experience. In fact, it would not be possible to have a lucid dream without some sort of focused intent. Consequently, we must recognize that people who slip into lucid dreams without significant programming have a conscious desire on some deep level to leave the physical body in a voyage of discovery and insight. In this manner, even they begin with some intent.

The lucid dream in all its vividness ushers the dreamer to situations, places, and times that are desired on a higher level with intent and driven by the causal energy body. The causal body is keenly focused on intent, purpose, cause, and effect. It is that part of us that is probably the most intuitive and all-knowing, sensing the purpose and intent behind all things. It is a creative force for truly knowing on an intimate level beyond the superficial understanding that most people accept as purely physical beings.

Once the lucid dreamer has arrived at a scene or situation, he or she is likely to witness other characters interacting as visitors outside normal time and space. Such dreamers are likely to observe themselves at an earlier or later stage or perhaps in another lifetime. Hence, the lucid dreamer becomes a witness with acute awareness and superconsciousness.

The vivid encounters one experiences in a lucid dream can be programmed with intent that is even vague in its desire to see beyond the superficial. Consequently, the discovery and insight we might seek in a programmed lucid dream can be vaguely drawn in the dreamer's preflight program that sets up the dream. You can ask for specific dream elements that will provide insight into certain things without knowing exactly where or when to search. Your conscious awareness as your guiding spirit of intelligent energy will find it for you. It innately knows where you have been, why you are here, and what your special purpose and mission in life is. This is your true self, your inner self that knows you better than you know your own face.

How Real Is My Dream?

The reality of our dreams is something that most people probably ponder most. It might seem vivid, but was it real? We tend to weigh vividness, by contrast, as simply an impression we have about something we witness. Whether it was, in fact, real is another tall bar to surpass for most of us.

We must evaluate at the outset the very nature of reality. How can we ever truly know what is real? Philosophers and scientists alike have pondered this question for centuries. I believe that if it seemed real to you and you acted upon it and participated in it, then the event was for all practical purposes real. That would hold true of dreams.

I am basing this position largely on the works of noted Polish philosopher and author Henryk Skolimowski, author of *Theatre of the Mind*. He focused his studies and writing on logic and the philosophy of language. Skolimowski spoke about one's moving reality, where we own the scene and observe moving parts with full consciousness and heightened awareness. That would certainly rule out imagination but include events and scenes where we are fully aware and own the scene as part of our moving reality.

In simple dreams of a restless mind during routine sleep cycles or daydreams, the scenes we review are nothing more than memories or copies of previously recorded information. It is like watching a movie inside your head. It might seem like moving reality but is actually a shadowy memory or impression of something that previously occurred. You are not moving or interacting, but simply reviewing an impression of something that your restless mind cannot let go. You might seem to interact in a different way each time you review your impression of this stored memory, but you have a limited scope of action or movement in this dream scenario. Any slight variation in the playback memory is a feeble attempt of the half-asleep mind to analyze and resolve what keeps it awake while the rest of you tries to sleep.

I do not mean to downplay the importance of your restless mind's concern over a memory, because it was real at one point and presents something your analytical mind desperately wants to resolve. But when you are sleeping, the idling brain that keeps resurfacing these impressions of past events cannot effectively analyze and resolve issues that trouble it. That simply brings these past memories to your attention, to demonstrate concern that you have not addressed it properly. Think of it as a desperate call for help. Only a fool would criticize having an alarm system or ignore its warnings during trouble. But the mind when half asleep during routine sleep is little more than an alarm with a vague sort of security camera that plays back a sketchy, blurred recording of the event in question.

The Reality of a Lucid Dream

By contrast, a lucid dream is more than a memory. Of course, it can be constructed on the basis of characters, events, scenes, and times that seem important to you, on the basis of prior experience. The new dream, however, will go beyond the static playback recording of a mental memory and explore new reality. A lucid dream builds new events and interaction and is not based totally on a stored physical memory of a past event or past concern.

Lucid dreams advance a storyline, with you fully present and engaged with other characters and situations, with acute awareness and superhuman abilities. Because a lucid dream takes you outside your head and outside your physical body, you are no longer limited by the normal laws of physics. You are no longer grounded to one place and time. You can roam and fly anywhere and anytime, no longer restricted by physical limitations.

Your consciousness soars in a nonphysical body of intelligent energy to deal with situations with heightened awareness. It takes you to new places beyond our physical limitations of three-dimensional, linear thinking, and five physical senses used for perception.

This dreamscape is as real as it gets, with you intimately present and absorbed in the scene as an onlooker. This is a new reality that you have discovered by journeying outside your dim memories and outside normal time and space. Whereas a common dream of a restless mind during sleep offers us a time capsule for review, a lucid dream takes us outside time and space for new adventures in discovery beyond what our physical body has experienced.

When your higher consciousness leaves your physical body, it is free to roam, explore, and discover to create new realities where you are not restricted by the confines of your physical mind and body and not limited by the physical limitations of time and space. It is not restricted to this moment in time as the only time you are focused on. It is not restricted to this place on which your physical body remains. It can explore new realities and limited space in an expanded multiple-universe of limitless potential.

In a lucid dream, your consciousness as pure energy moves in the spirit realm of unmanifested energy beyond the manifest physical level of creation. In this new rarified air, it can effect change quickly without the restriction of a slowed-down realm of fixed structure.

It is perhaps ironic that a person can become fully awake and alive only when physically asleep in a lucid dream.

CHAPTER 4

Beyond Rapid Eye Movement into Real Movement

Medical science always seems ready to argue for a purely mechanical or material reductionist explanation for everything in our lives. It likes to study rapid eye movement (REM) in sleeping subjects. I will apologize at the outset here if I offend you as someone who puts much faith in such scientific measurements, but I find it personally flawed that true unbiased research of any kind must depend on a mechanical explanation. That approach simply ignores how manifest energy in the physical realm is infused with energy at all levels, including our whole being. It overlooks how electromagnetic energy or intelligent energy commonly known as consciousness exists outside physical measurement as a driving and sustaining force in all life. But if you cannot see it, weigh it, or measure its size, then it does not *appear* to exist in our physical world, according to medical science.

If we are going to seriously discuss human dreaming here, however, we also must review the medical research based on rapid-eye-movement study of dreamers during sleep. Let us put that review under careful consideration by first eliminating what lucid dream is *not* in our quest to learn what lucid dreaming truly *is*.

Medical research, generally speaking, attempts to study what happens during our normal sleep patterns in physical terms. This is based on physical science and allopathic medicine, which is conditioned to accept a simple physiological explanation for everything we experience. These dedicated, well-meaning researchers try to eliminate physiological explanations for the human experience before ever considering supernatural or esoteric answers. They do not accept the concept of subtle energy bodies or superconsciousness as intelligent energy as part of our makeup beyond basic anatomy and physiology.

Common dreams that are remembered generally will occur during rapid eye movement (REM activity), according to neurological research. Study in this area indicates that most people commonly dream about two hours in an average night throughout a lifetime, although most dreams last only five to twenty minutes. Most people are not even aware that they are dreaming, since the prefrontal cortex or area of the brain associated with logic and planning exhibits less activity during dreaming. As a result, people typically can interact within a common dream without much analysis within the swirling blur of dream imagery.

Dreams during REM become longer throughout the night, as people go deeper into sleep mode. First dreams of the night might last only ten minutes, but the dream episodes increase to approximately twenty minutes later in sleep. Curiously, people who experience common REM dreams cannot accurately determine the length of their dreams, since the passage of time is apparently hard to determine in our dreams.

REM research would suggest that many animals experience dreaming—not just human beings. Science has observed what appears to be dreaming in all mammals studied and has also reported signs that dreaming occurs in reptiles and birds. It would seem from this biological research that sleeping and common dreaming are intertwined.

Biological research into the common dreams that occur with rapid eye movement in deep sleep suggests that chemical changes in the body during normal sleep mode induce dreaming. This supposition gains ground, perhaps, with studies that show how certain chemicals ingested just prior to sleep will interfere with typical REM dream activity. Certain drugs appear to block typical chemical reactions within the body during sleep and halt routine dreaming. On the other hand, certain drugs such as dopamine seem to stimulate excessive vivid dreaming during REM activity and even increase nightmares.

It is important to note that study of rapid eye movement in various deep levels of sleep throughout the night examines common dreams that randomly occur to most people during routine sleep periods. These are not the same as lucid dreams that are induced or programmed in a more conscious state of heightened awareness, as in a waking dream. It is not the same as the dream walking of shamanic cultures induced during a vision quest, or the same as yogi masters, such as Samadhi mystics, in programmed lucid dreaming.

Rapid eye movement in dream research simply measures physical eye twitches as telltale signs that the psyche is processing deep memories in the physical brain. In this manner, our psychological concerns are replayed and rehashed by a restless mind that is not fully asleep during physical rest periods.

One leading scientific researcher, Eugen Tarnow (author of *Working Memory Capacities Differ by Academic Fields* and *Serial Position Curve of Free Recall Repeats*), suggests that dreams can be explained as simply excitations of long-term memory. He says that our brain executive function seeks to interpret long-term memory to check its consistency with how we view reality.

Tarnow's analysis fits with views of psychotherapist Sigmund Freud where he examines the role of the subconscious in dream analysis. Dr. Freud in the late nineteenth century declared that many of our dreams are driven by subconscious wish fulfillment. Freud theorized, upon clinical observation, that important subconscious desires relate to early-childhood memories and experiences.

Freud initially interpreted many dreams as sexual in nature. He also considered possible supernatural roots for many of these subconscious memories. Many of Freud's earlier patients, he thought, suffered from chronic nightmares or childhood disorders. That led Freud to describe a dark pattern in many dreams. He felt that such dreams were rooted in psychological disorders. Freud then attempted to analyze these dark, psychological disorders behind dreams through interpretation of recurring images and symbols in such dreams. Dream imagery as interpretation of our dreams has become popular in our age, and much of it stems from Dr. Freud's probing into dark psychological disorders.

Later, Freud decided that it would be impossible to classify many of these psychological dreams as wish fulfillment, and his earlier views on dreams were discarded by many in the profession. Indeed, more-modern dream research tends to debunk Freud's dream theories. Also discarded today is the Freudian theory that dreams serve as guardians of required sleep.

His view that dreams have coherence and connect the dreamer to recent waking thoughts in some circumstances continues to enjoy some support in modern dream research. And the Freudian basic interest in dream interpretation continues to enjoy popularity today.

Depth psychologist Carl Jung rejected many of Freud's views in describing dreams. He saw potentially significant messages in dreams that the dreamer should take seriously. Jung felt that dreams present the dreamer with revelations that are useful in resolving emotional issues, spiritual concerns, and personal fears. Recurring dreams, he said, demand attention to something the person is ignoring in life. He urged people to observe symbols and images that are repeated in dreams. We see a more mystical, esoteric approach in Jung's work.

Fritz Perls, author of *Gestalt Therapy*, takes an even more holistic approach to dreams, seeing them as projections of elements of the whole self that have been repressed or rejected. Whereas Jung believed that every person whom you see in your dream is an extension of you, Perls suggests that even inanimate objects in your dream represent aspects of you as dreamer. When dreamers recognize these objects of aspects of personal character, then they become more aware of these characteristics in their personality.

That brings our scientific survey of dreams to neurological research. Allan Hobson, author of *Dream Consciousness*, and Robert McCarley, coauthor of *Brain Control of Wakefulness and Sleep*, have challenged the Freudian view of dreams as subconscious wishes to be interpreted. Their new neurological view suggests that signals interpreted by dreams originate in the brain stem where circuits are activated during rapid eye movement (REM) sleep patterns. An evolution of this theory suggests that the brain is the inducer of dreams in downloading stored memories into deep memory banks. Such dreaming, therefore, is maintained by the dreamer's own thinking.

Neurologists and other medical researchers maintain that our physical brain is the magnificent engine of every thought, action, and reaction that occurs in our lives, of course. They cannot acknowledge what they cannot readily see or measure physically. This overlooks past-life flashbacks and out-of-body descriptions that many people seem to have in near-death experiences or medical incidents when a person is brain dead and yet functioning on some superhuman level of consciousness.

There is, sadly, an expression for the futile efforts of people who keep trying the same approach over and over in hopes of finding new results, just as there is an expression for people who keep hitting their heads against brick walls in attempts to achieve a breakthrough. We call that shortsighted or scanning a problem only superficially. Why not accept the probability that there exists a life force or spirit inside us on a nonphysical level with superconsciousness? Since electromagnetic energy drives and maintains all life around us, is it not reasonable to assume that such pure intelligent energy also resides within us? It would offer explanations to puzzling problems that anatomy and physiology seem incapable of resolving.

Perhaps we are truly awake only during lucid dreams or times when this conscious spirit or light within us escapes our physical confines during sleep. If a caterpillar can hide a butterfly, why can't we? In the ancient-wisdom tradition, this was called transformation or going beyond the physical form to a higher form.

CHAPTER 5

What Can I Accomplish or Realize from My Dream?

People often believe that whatever odd or amazing insight they discover in a dream displays some sort of fluke or drifting vision that somehow floated their way. Others proudly proclaim that all their dream insights and discoveries are gifts of the spirit or divine revelation. They credit little personal involvement in setting up the dream and personally engineering its direction.

That is the case of common dreams of a restless brain that keeps sorting through concerns and situations it cannot seem to resolve during moments when fully awake and analyzing the way our mind does in filing memories. There is no real preparation or direction to the dream that comes to us in restless nights of ordinary dreaming.

Even lucid dreams that we somehow slip into without prior planning could seem somewhat random and without much meaning. Of course, the conscious mind can occasionally thrust us into a vivid dream that is lucid and revealing with much detail. It can even hold great insight, since our conscious mind has greater powers than our restless brain in sorting through matters of concern.

We cannot, then, overlook the importance of random and unplanned lucid dreams. The spirit within us leads us toward self-examination and realization of truths that are not obvious to the physical side of us. Sometimes the hidden self that dwells within us seizes an opportunity when the physical body and brain slow down to enter a rest cycle. There is nothing holding it back, then, if the brain is truly in retreat as the gatekeeper of everything and everyone.

Programmed lucid dreams as serious dreamwork, however, offer us a wealth of possible accomplishments and realizations based on the task list that we build into the process. We can literally outline where we want to go, who we want to see, the situation or scene we want to review, and what we desire to learn. This might seem grandiose and a lot to expect from a dream, but people around the world have been doing serious dreamwork with planned expectations for centuries. This is a minority of people, of course, composed of forward-thinking people who are in touch with their inner selves, with an understanding of the power of human consciousness.

In this chapter, then, we will review the way that a person can self-direct a lucid dream for maximum benefit. We also will examine the random lucid dream, which can be gleaned for insights after the fact if we lean to internalize our dreams carefully.

First, let us properly examine what insights might be taken from a common dream of a restless brain. We do not outright dismiss such normal dreams—as colorless and chaotic as they might appear—since they offer insights into our subconscious mind that is preoccupied with matters it cannot let go, even during sleep. These concerns that we cannot let rest keep bubbling up from our restless mind, showing the importance we give them. Their continual resurfacing also shows how troubled we are by these concerns or how psychologically tangled we find ourselves in dealing with them. These might be flights of fancy, obsessions, or desires as much as things that vex us. They represent things we need to resolve.

Consequently, these recurring common dreams of a restless mind offer insights to what concerns us psychologically. A good psychologist, psychotherapist, or psychiatrist might help you analyze these dreams and work your way through them to greater insight. Some people even try to analyze their own common dreams of the restless mind by consulting dream dictionaries. These dreams are highly personal, however, so it becomes questionable whether another person's coded imagery has the same meaning for you. If you want to find insight in a common dream of your restless mind, you might consider personally meditating on it to determine your own special message, if there is one.

After a common dream, I like to stay in bed with eyes shut and enter into a reflecting meditation where I get in touch with my body on all levels. In this state of body awareness, I can more easily hold on to the recent dream and review it. Then I can begin to let it sink into my mind to see where it fits and how it feels. Ideally, I can analyze it. After I have done that, I will slowly get out of bed, trying to hold on to the dream review and sit near my bed to jot down what I remember in a dream journal. After producing an outline of the dream on paper, I might try to analyze it in a fully awake condition, sitting by my dream journal.

Often, these common dreams are just the wandering of a restless mind, without much point or focus. They do, however, suggest what is important to you as something you need to resolve. So maybe we should look positively on these common dreams of a night of tossing and turning for what they can offer us on a psychological level. We might see them, then, as a window to the psyche.

But if common dreams offer a view of our inner psyche, then the lucid dream on the grander scale of higher consciousness offers us a window to our soul. This is where our inner spirit resides. This is the secret home where the true self that dwells within us hides out of view, just waiting for the opportunity to spring forward.

What Random Lucid Dreams Offer Us

A random lucid dream, while unplanned and not programmed, nonetheless offers us great opportunity of discovery and insight. After all, such a vivid dream is the work of our heightened consciousness, freed from the restraints of our body and mind with all the innate knowledge and vision of an old soul. This energized intelligence is our eternal self, carefully wrapped inside a cocoon of dense physical matter that is directed by a little brain that automates what our body needs to do to survive in a manifest reality. You can accomplish much in even a random lucid dream and realize much from the experience that unfolds before you in that dream state.

The key to unraveling an unplanned lucid dream is processing it after the fact. Whereas dreamwork plans a specific assignment in the dreamscape, an unplanned lucid dream needs to be carefully reconstructed after the dream has ended. As a gift of spirit, it should be unloaded and handled upon reentry to the physical body with due reverence and respect for what it might likely contain for you in your growth. At an inner core level, you desired to embark on this journey of discovery in a lucid dream, obviously knowing at a deep level that it could hold something key to your life, something that you were not able to discern and sort out on a mundane level when you were physically in motion with your brain cranking away at questions and concerns.

This random lucid dream, while unplanned, therefore represents your soul's urgent desire to provide you with insight that can guide you in your life journey in ways that somehow evade your physical level of understanding as hidden and deep. Think of consciousness jumping out of you as the perfect troubleshooter who knows you better than you think you know yourself during waking moments. Think of consciousness, not only coming to the rescue to put you on course, but as a prophet. This all-knowing, all-seeing prophet can take you through strange, uncharted terrain and find your way to the point of discovery and then take you safely home. This is your conscious connection to divine source, the alpha and the omega, the light of the world that feeds all sparks of light throughout creation, including your own divine flame that burns within you.

When consciousness takes you on a journey of discovery in an unplanned lucid dream, it is because it knows what you want and knows what you need on a fundamental level. It knows the past and knows the future and understands where you are on the arc of your own life journey in relation to where you should be. It perceives the need to orient you and set you straight, so it leaps into action—not because you asked, but because you urgently need it.

This special dream, then, is the work of the fire within you, your connection to the eternal flame. Think of the trinity inside us, waiting to be connected. We see a triangle of body, mind, and soul. The soul is your heightened consciousness that completes you as dynamic life force. It is driven by desire, innate understanding, and acute awareness. When we put our emotional and mental subtle energy bodies together with our causal body of desire and innate knowing, we connect the energetic connection within us with the power of an internal pyramid. When we stand back from the pyramid and admire it from afar, we see a triangle that is grounded. The meaning of the word *pyramid* as *fire within a geometric shape* indicates the sacred geometry and hidden power within our very core bodies. The fire within you has given you new insight in the form of a lucid dream.

Unpacking an unexpected lucid dream can take time and might occur over many recurrences of the same or similar dreamscape brought to your attention. Why is spirit showing this to you? What does it mean? How does it impact your life? You will need patience to sort it all out upon reentry, to be sure.

The basic approach that I recommend for understanding a random lucid dream is much the same as the approach outlined above for a random common dream that is not lucid. When the dream ends and you begin to return to normal physical consciousness, remain still in the same position, with eyes closed. Try to delay your full reentry to normal physical consciousness as long as possible with your eyes shut. Hold on to the dream as best you can for as long as you can. Do not stir or move any part of your body, since that only places you back into your physical body and disconnects you from the dreamscape.

Let the dream wash over you without analyzing it. This is very esoteric, I know, but the dream itself was a voyage of your spirit and not psychological. Allow the meaning of the dream to impact you on all levels of your whole being. Think of this as *gnosis* or inner knowing beyond any exoteric meaning or significance. There is a connotative meaning as well as a denotative meaning to profound truth, and what spirit has given you is profound truth, if you can discern it.

Just as the dreamscape has finished washing throughout your whole being, enter a meditative state to grasp it. Do this by keeping your body still and numb. Do not engage the senses or your presence in the physical room that surrounds you. Do not begin thinking of the dream in depth, since that only engages the physical brain in analysis, which it is incapable of doing here. Begin deep, rhythmic breathing through the nostrils. Focus on one nostril at first and then switch to the other nostril. Do not engage any sense of touch or feel in the body but remain in this meditative state.

Now picture a clean, blank slate inside you and direct your inner eye upon that slate with focused intent. Visualize the dream experience on that slate. You will draw or paint upon the slate without words or thoughts. Just examine it. Continue to gaze upon it without comment or conjecture. See it as a scene you observed, much like the frozen frame of a movie.

Stay with this picture as long as you can before rising from your resting position. When you open your eyes and stand, the picture will fade. This is not like processing your reentry from the common random dream that is not lucid, because it does not involve the psyche in the way your analytical brain tries to sort things out for you. This is not a psychological dream, but a dream of the spirit, outside the scope of your simple physical experience and the domain of your brain as memory bank and process center.

This is not a dream that a psychologist is likely to help you understand, since it is beyond the psychology of your mind as a gift of the spirit. It needs to be unwrapped and treated with sensitivity on a personal level as a private message that only you can hope to comprehend on some level. If you do ultimately elect to jot down the dream in a dream journal, simply outline the scene, characters, and events without attempting to analyze them in your writing. Your analytical brain was not present at this dream, and sorting out a dream of heightened consciousness out of body is beyond its pay grade. Nonetheless, you might want to outline a pattern of recurring dreams of a lucid nature. This might begin to make sense to you on a deeper level.

Your random lucid dream has likely taken you places of great teaching and insight. It has likely taken you outside normal physical space and time of the here and now. It has likely shown you mysteries about the nature of life and your own life mission and purpose that you have hidden inside you, somewhat forgotten at birth but burning inside you like a flame that cannot be ignored.

Ignore this gift of spirit at your own peril! Discarded insights and discoveries on this level have consequences. If you acknowledge the gift and hold it dear, your lucid dream will continue in a pattern of vivid dreams that show you over and over what you need to know. The recurring dreams might vary slightly, since consciousness serves you the message in variations intended to connect with you one way or another in an ongoing process.

That is the way that karma works on a personal level, putting the opportunity in front of you again and again in repetitive fashion or with slight variation to connect with you. These dreams are instructive on a deep, cosmic level to bring you in line with your own special purpose and place in the grand scheme of things.

Internalizing the message as best you are able will position you to achieve greater depth in future lucid dreams. These increasingly deep dreams likely will follow a recurring pattern. Ignoring a lucid dream by not internalizing the message will not necessarily stop the flow of lucid dreams in this area. Karma will work to get your attention. Such ignored dreams will thunder home the message to you in various ways. It will resemble the movie *Groundhog Day*, where a person is forced to repeat the same experience over and over, day after day, until the message is fully internalized and understood.

Gifts of a Programmed Lucid Dream

Self-directed, planned lucid dreams can offer us more in what they accomplish for us and what we can realize as a result. Serious dreamworking begins with an agenda of precisely what you want to experience and learn in your dream, on the basis of your early mapping of the dreamscape before departing.

The mapping that I advocate involves visualizing a picture on a blank screen before your mind's eye before departing on your lucid dream. It does not matter how exacting your drawing might appear. You will understand it and use it as a map to direct you wherever your conscious energy takes you. Your picture can be a crude stick drawing if you are not very artistic, like me. Or you can embellish it by painting something in exotic colors. The point is that you have created a map that you can tuck into your consciousness to take you exactly where you want to go.

Since you are leaving normal time and space in a purely energy body, you can go literally anywhere you desire. You can go back in time or forward in time. You can select out-of-this-world destinations if you choose. You can pick the people you want to see and the situations you want to visit. These can be events in time or situations that you want to explore in a dreamscape.

You will go there as a perfect witness, not interacting with others as you observe them. You might observe yourself from a more objective point of view as witness to a scene. You are there to observe, learn, and grow. This can be an experience of great insight for you, this gift of the spirit.

Of course, your spirit in its role of director might edit your map a little if it considers that important and timely for your life journey of discovery. Think of the Lord Krishna's role in ushering Arjuna on his chariot in the Hindu classic *The Bhagavad Gita*. Krishna consciousness is precisely what we are talking about here: our divine connection to cosmic insight. We are looking for the meaning and significance beneath the surface of our superficial, material world.

This is the arc of your own hero's journey, where supernatural encounters challenge the would-be hero with gates to negotiate, supernatural obstacles to be overcome, and mentors who offer direction toward transformation and eventual wholeness. Think of your planned lucid dream as a supernatural journey toward personal enlightenment. This is a lofty goal that might take you several lifetimes. Fortunately, lucid dreams offer you a supernatural portal through time and space to help get you there, one journey at a time.

And since you have planned this adventure in lucid dreaming with specific objectives, you are likely to be acutely aware during your voyage of discovery and know precisely what you can expect to find. Upon returning from your dream, you will not be disoriented as in a common dream of a restless mind or even a random, unplanned lucid dream. Consequently, you will be able to internalize the experience and bring the insight home with you. Think of this as careful planning for an important journey where you hope to see and learn many things.

In any important journey, the traveler with great expectation packs carefully and plans the journey. This requires your focused intent. When we direct our heightened consciousness with such focused intent, we can target many significant things in our travel and return with great insight.

The programmed lucid dream can be mapped to show you what you need to know about your past, people who have had an impact on your life, impactful events that require greater understanding, and much more. We can return to ourselves at an earlier age to help heal ourselves in the present. We can project ourselves into what we call our future to see how the course of our life thus far seems to be leading us. Space and time are not physical barriers to pure consciousness that leaves our body in a lucid dream.

As mentioned earlier, upon return the completion of the journey as programmed by ourselves should prove easy to unpack. As with common dreams and even random lucid dreams, the dreamer in a self-directed lucid dream should remain at rest with eyes closed upon return from a dream to hold the image of the experience as long as possible and meditate upon it. Then the dreamer might slowly rise to jot down the outline and basics of the dream without analysis. On a deeper level, you innately know what you have encountered, because you were acutely aware. This dream was not an accident but a planned excursion into deeper awareness.

CHAPTER 6

Preparing for a Dream Journey

As we have seen, preparation for a self-directed lucid dream is the key to making the experience meaningful and insightful. That is the primary purpose of this book. The next chapter will take you deeper into the preparation for a planned, self-programmed lucid dream. While people for centuries have called this dreamwork, we should also look at it as a thrilling ride to places of discovery many people never experience.

Basically, there are three phases to programming your own lucid dreams. They follow my teacher Louis Gittner's three-stage magical formula for manifesting new reality: *Conceive, achieve, and believe.* Since I have given you the magical formula of Louis, I feel that I should tell you a little about him and his magical life on beautiful Orcas Island in the San Juans. Louis ran an inn there that he remodeled, adding a chapel in back. His gardens were amazing, with perfect flowers of immense size and life. He wrote several esoteric books on living, including *There Is a Rainbow, Love Is a Verb*, and *Listen, Listen, Listen*.

Otherwise, he led a rather quiet, private life at the inn except when would-be students would discover him and ask for help. When Louis went into his own version of a lucid dream, light shone upon him in a darkened room, and he would listen to conscious energy all around him. He was able to communicate to others what he learned from this conscious energy. He confirmed what he had learned from the energized consciousness around him by traveling to Findhorn in Scotland to compare his diary entries with those of Dorothy Maclean. They determined that they were receiving the same messages at the same time, accounting for time zone differences. That certainly explained why both the Findhorn Garden and the garden of his inn were so amazing.

Consequently, when Louis told me to always remember to listen and to follow his three-part formula for realizing energetic transformation, I took special note. Throughout the years, since I first met him at his inn decades ago, I have tried to internalize his primary message and sort it out. I will try to do that for you here.

Conceptualize Your Intent

The first thing to do in manifesting transformation in your life and attaining a new reality is to *conceive* what you intend to bring forward in your life. You need to focus the energized consciousness of your mental, emotional, and causal subtle bodies to do this.

In self-directing a lucid dream, you need to conceive of what you intend to achieve, observe, or learn in your voyage of discovery. Consider this the all-important planning phase for programming your adventure in the dreamscape. As with every great journey, you must plan what you want to discover, where you plan to go, and what scenes and characters you wish to encounter there. You are your own travel agent, and the sky is the limit.

I always caution people in setting up a lucid dream to avoid normal analytical thought. The first thing you need to do before you can carefully and creatively plan your dream is to put your entire physical body to sleep, including your brain. Now, the brain must continue to direct the flow of blood and oxygen through the body and assume control over the normal body functions that will keep you alive and safe during your lucid dream. It does not need to be actively engaged in planning or participating in a lucid dream. Consequently, it can go into a rest phase when it only directs and administers anatomical functions of our physiology during repose.

So, to do this, follow these steps:

- Recline on your back in a bed or on the floor, with a mat or blanket as cushion. Wear loose-fitting, comfortable clothing with all shoes, socks, and jewelry removed. Extend your legs and arms at 45-degree angles in the so-called dead-man position familiar to students of yoga. This also could be done in a straight-back chair with erect posture and bare feet solidly grounded, although a reclining position usually proves better.
- Focus on putting your feet to sleep by sending the message that they are heavy and need to grow numb and rest. Then, do the same with other parts of our body, working your way up the legs, torso, chest, arms, and head. When you feel your nose, chin, ears, and scalp grow numb, then recognize that the physical body has been put to rest.
- Begin deep, rhythmic breathing, conscious of the energy in each breath you take in, process, and expel with your blessing. You might initially count slowly to three while taking in new breath, holding the breath inside for three seconds with the realization that you have been

energized by it, and then slowly exhaling it with a blessing for three seconds. Do this until it becomes automatic, without counting to three for each of the three phases.
- You are getting ready to put your physical mind to rest, a necessary step that requires internal harmony between your physical brain and higher consciousness to allow the simple mind to go into a rest phase. At this point, the mind surrenders control with the assurance that your physical self will be safe and rested during your lucid dream outside the body.
- At this point, tune out all external and internal distractions, including sensory perception and inner thoughts. You are sensing a dimness in your brain function. It should not be thinking or processing. Meanwhile, your heightened consciousness, as an aspect of your inner spirit, is beginning to assume control, operating at an accelerated speed.
- You see a blank slate in front of your mind's eye and nothing else. On this slate, begin to visualize what you intend to experience in the lucid dream ahead of you, when your consciousness is ready to depart the physical body to explore outside normal space and time. This is your shopping list on a different sort of trip to the market. This is what you most want from your lucid dream. You can make this as detailed or simple as you want. You will be able to read the list, since it is written in your own special handwriting in pictographs. Include anything you want to learn or experience.
- Now, if you get to this point in programming your lucid dream but still are experiencing internal distractions of a restless mind, physical sensations, or outside distractions, then recognize that you are not prepared to enter a lucid dream. In such case, begin again to put the body and mind to sleep, establish proper breathing, and enter the blank space inside you before your mind's eye. This is a deep meditation and not a superficial mediation to experience body connection.
- If you are setting up a posthypnotic suggestion to enter a lucid dreamscape upon entering normal sleep, then you need to do that now. Consequently, the next step after creating your picture map inside you is slightly different depending on the type of lucid dream you intend to have—during sleep or as a waking dream (not during sleep time).
- If you want to experience a self-programmed lucid dream during your evening of sleep, absorb the map you have drawn on the clean slate before your mind's eye. Then consciously tuck it into the back of your consciousness, with the intent to recall it when you enter sleep phase. Focus your intent to automatically recall the map and then follow it in a dream voyage outside the physical body, beyond normal time and

space. This posthypnotic suggestion should include permission for you to leave the physical body as soon as you enter sleep phase.

This lucid dream during normal sleep time should satisfy the inherent human desire to dream during sleep, as sleep therapists sometimes warn us is a concern for emotional and mental health. As a bonus, the approach will leave your body completely rested, unlike in common restless dreams, and not stress your psyche with the sort of psychological unrest that often comes with common restless sleep dreams. As an added bonus, you are experiencing lucid dreaming efficiently during sleep periods and not during the course of your busy day.

The other approach, of course, is to set up a waking dream by tucking the image of the map you have drawn on the blank screen before your mind's eye to instantly recall on command. You can simply focus your intent with the full power of your will to follow that map as soon as you have completed it, leaving the body to explore a vivid dreamscape outside normal time and space. Finishing the map can trigger the intent to immediately leave the physical body, using the map as an unerring guide to where you want to go. In such case, you should project in a conscious energy body to precisely that location with precisely those situations that you have selected. Your spirit knows the way and needs only your focused intent to dispatch it with the speed and accuracy of a karmic arrow that draws a straight line directly from your physical location to the dreamscape location you have selected. Think of this as two ends of a magnet that are instantly and powerfully connected. This is electromagnetic energy in a karmic sense, connecting you to another side of you.

In the beginning, you might want to examine the map you have drawn and then tuck it into the back of your memory as you prepare yourself with the command of your will to leave the body to that designated dreamscape when you recall the map to the screen in front of your mind's eye. As you practice programming your lucid dreams, however, this added step of storing to prepare for departure might become less necessary, as you become more accustomed to leaving the physical body on cue with focus.

Reaching Your Goals in a Lucid Dream

The second step of the three-part magical formula—to *achieve*—is realized when you reach and experience your lucid dreamscape and address the goals you have intended. Of course, we will recognize here that spirit might alter the goals of this voyage of discovery, since it knows best what you need to learn and experience. When it is given freedom to show you the way, it will course-correct as needed. So do not become upset if your goals drawn on your blank screen are slightly altered along the way. Spirit listens, but spirit also corrects our course for our own good. So make the most of the experience and try to learn and grow with insights you are given in the dreamscape.

Abandon the concept we have in our physical lives of directing every little thing to effect change and trigger responses. This is not a play that you have written, and certainly not a play in which you star as an actor. Rather, think of your good fortune to score a ticket to this play as an audience member.

We spend so much time and energy in our physical lives trying to master cause and effect with words and action that we somehow expect will result in alterations in the fabric of things. We seem to stumble around in our clumsy physical bodies with our pea-size brains with half-hearted attempts to cause transition and ultimately transformation. We seem to crave true understanding of how karma works and how energy reinvents itself in many forms. You will not interact in your lucid dream or alter events in the past or future. But you have a golden opportunity given to you by the freedom of spirit loosed by consciousness to observe and learn how things develop, if only you will acutely focus your awareness in the dreamscape.

Begin by orienting yourself and assuring yourself of your real presence as soon as you arrive at the dreamscape. Look at the back of your hands to sense your conscious presence. (You will have a sort of etheric body of some nonphysical form that resembles your physical body but is pure energy.) Scan the scene carefully, observing every nuance from the characters assembled, the place, the time, and the scene that is unfolding. Maybe you will see yourself there in another time and place. Carefully absorb the details down to the color of things, like a fly on the wall.

In our mundane lives as physical creatures, we try to alter the nature of things in many ways—from churning cream into butter, shaping trees, and building bookshelves. In the grand scheme of creation, these minute changes represent small change to matter that nonetheless remains matter in a slightly different form that suits us for the moment. Here in the lucid dreamscape, you will alter how things unfold as a perfect witness with acute awareness. You are here to learn and grow, hopefully bringing insight back to you in the here and now. So, listen, see, and feel everything in that lucid dream intently so you can internalize the message.

There are specific things that you desired to observe in your dreamscape, ideally providing insight that is deep and transformational. Added to your planned list are gifts of the spirit that your inner self knew were important to your development. You should look carefully with acute awareness at what unfolds before your new eyes in the dreamscape, observing characters, events, and situations that can impact your life. Your lucid dream should not end until you have observed all points of interest in your self-directed dream of discovery. It is possible that you will end your dream early if you fail to observe all points of interest and are simply drifting through the dreamscape with little focus. Of course, you can always program the same dream and return to try again.

Internalizing What You Have Learned

The third phase is *believing* what you have conceived and achieved in your out-of-body lucid dream of discovery. Every good adventurer should bring back knowledge and insight from the journey. Every arc of the hero's journey traditionally includes treasures that the hero has won and brought home. When you truly accept something that you have observed as real and meaningful to you on a deeper level, you believe it fully. This is more than simply taking notice of something and then tucking it away somewhere as something you have seen. This is more than having belief in a cause, person, or way of looking at things as something that you can accept. It is taking it deep inside you and absorbing it as part of the wholeness of your being. It becomes an active and integral part of you.

In communication, this is generally called internalizing the message. Here, the internal consumption and importance of what you have consumed means more to you. It becomes a part of you, a key part. In our busy lives as mundane physical creatures in a social environment with others who have an impact on us daily, we take in countless messages from all around us without much significance. It is rare, perhaps, whenever someone absorbs information that changes how they see things and how they live their lives.

We just do not believe that profoundly in many things within the vast profusion of information that is thrust at us indiscriminately. In the first place, this glut of information is not particularly targeted at us or for us. It does not necessarily have our best interests at heart. I recall participating in an advanced communication class at the University of Washington in the processing of international communication data. The research group was headed by a senior professor who had gathered data abroad about how people in various cultures utilize information. He found that very few people use mass media information on a personal level to determine their sense of reality and guide their political decisions. It just does not register that deeply as something they truly believe.

The second point that should be made here in this comparison concerns how information given to people in a common scattergun approach to communication dissemination is not personally targeted. Consequently, it begins life with little intent. As the communication is absorbed and processed, then, it has even less intent attached to it. It is simply not impactful. It does not help define you, your values, or your sense of direction. It does not associate with who you are and how you see yourself. It is simply not for you.

On the arc of the hero's journey, the traveler traditionally faces challenges, overcomes obstacles, and undergoes supernatural pitfalls that can catapult the traveler to new heights of awareness as a transformed person. Traditionally, the arc of the journey takes the hero to the depths of despair at a halfway point, often seen as the point of no return. Absorbing the lessons of this abyss in the darkest hour of the soul, some heroes with proper motivation and awareness emerge from the abyss as new people, transformed by the experience. The road is an arduous place of discovery with lessons for those who are prepared.

Now we all know people around us—people who stumble through life, who seem to have many challenging situations tossed at them in ways that offer them a chance to learn and grow from their life experiences. This is the way the road looks to all of us—filled with challenges, obstacles, and life-altering life lessons along the way. But somehow, they fail to learn and grow with these experiences presented to them. That is the physical road of life that most of us recognize in our waking hours as mundane creatures.

They simply do not outline what they want to experience to bring situations when they want them. Not only do they not conceive of learning from their life experiences, but they absorb information only from experiences that they see as troubling and confusing. Making matters ever worse, they do not believe that the life lessons thrust at them to provide them with insight had any significance to process and internalize.

Lessons of the lucid dream, therefore, might be wasted on them. They are not looking to learn, attain, and grow internally. They are not ready to build the inner self to prepare it for its continuing journey of evolution, because they do not recognize the fire within them as an eternal spirit who longs to explore, learn, and grow. They are simply interested in creature comforts such as a good nap, a good snack, and an easy life with little movement. That is not the arc of a hero's journey and not the way the inner self sees itself. But they keep the inner self forever sleeping.

Our task here is to awaken the inner self and set it free to become more.

CHAPTER 7
Establishing Perfect Body, Mind, and Spirit Harmony

Not enough can be said here about the importance of establishing a harmony of body, mind, and spirit prior to entering a state of heightened consciousness to program an out-of-body lucid dream. Unless there is harmony, your protective physical mind will not allow it. Your brain assumes responsibility for your safety on all levels and is reluctant to ever surrender control even for a moment. It might not even recognize your heightened consciousness as outside itself. It might consider surrender to the consciousness and its own period of deeper rest as dangerous and foolhardy.

This gatekeeper obstacle long has been addressed by people who meditate in the East and in the West. In the yoga tradition, students of deeper meditation are taught to "slay the mind" to allow the consciousness to take one into a meditation outside its control. The Sanskrit translation of the word *slay* is perhaps unfortunate here. We do not want to actually kill the physical mind or defeat it, but only subdue it as gatekeeper to allow our consciousness to emerge while the physical brain stands down.

Your brain cannot take you where spirit needs to go. Your physical brain has insufficient memory banks and data at its disposal to handle such a meditation. A deep, active meditation, after all, takes place outside the physical realm in the spirit realm of unmanifested energy, far from the dense world of manifest energy familiar to our physical mind and body. This would be a little like asking a person who has always lived in an isolated village in France with no knowledge of the outside world or another language to suddenly travel alone in Spain.

Medical science, of course, might try to disagree that any higher intelligent energy could assert itself in our lives to replace the key control of the human brain over all activities. They seem to have a protective stance that nothing nonphysical appears at work in our lives beyond the anatomical and physiological components that are material. If they cannot measure it, weigh it, and see it to describe it, even under a microscope, then in their opinion it cannot possibly exist. They have a way of somehow explaining near-death experiences where the brain ceases to function for a while as still under the control of the brain. They explain out-of-body experiences as imagination of a creative mind. They explain people who suddenly speak a foreign language or play the piano without training as an amazing example of how the physical brain can glean bits of information and somehow process this information into surprising skills. But we must always remember that our physical brains are only as complete in their information banks with the data we have stored in them during our physical lives. They are limited to our physical memories.

No, we are looking for a higher consciousness as nonphysical pure energy that resides deep within us as part of an inner self or spirit within us. We cannot see it, measure it, or weigh it. It is hard for us to easily measure energy, since it has no material form. And yet, we all recognize sunshine and wind. When I go sailing with people who have never been aboard a sailboat, I see the amazement on their faces as the wind pulls us forward silently. It is much the same reaction I have when I stand in front of an array of solar reflectors at a site powered solely by the sun, since I grew up thinking of electricity coming only from noisy hydroelectric dams of immense size and power plants the size of baseball fields.

Perhaps people who are asked to meditate and surrender control to higher consciousness sense that as a loss of control. They are asked to trust something they cannot physically see or measure. They are asked to trust their inner spirit. I suspect that many people do not trust this inner spirit, because they do not feel that it is really a part of them. Perhaps they sense that they are losing control to some outside spirit.

Most of us are not told about our inner self, a higher self that dwells within us. It is something that some of us gradually begin to accept. The true self, most suppose, is the superficial reflection that we see in mirrors as light bouncing off our bodies. The true self, they suppose, is the collection of bones with muscles, tendons, tissue, and nerves that tie our whole bodies together with physical impulses to lift our legs, manipulate our delicate digits, and throw a ball across a distance on the fly with unerring accuracy.

What could be better than our physical selves? The materialist can imagine nothing else. And, truly, our physical bodies are amazing. But there is much more to our whole being than our anatomy and physiology. Where do we find our inner impulse and desire? Where do we find the intuition that alerts us to things even before they happen, or alert us to things around the corner? Obviously, there is more to us than meets the eye.

What we cannot readily see or accept as a hidden aspect of ourselves, however, is an uncomfortable notion for some people, who fear they are losing control. If this innate insight and ability is not part of them, they worry; then perhaps it is an outside force that has seized control over them! Is this spirit possession? It seems a terrible sense of insecurity to believe that you have lost control over your own life. If you do not understand that feeling, just consider elderly people who are put into nursing homes and heavily controlled throughout every moment of their day and night. Consider prisoners who have no freedom of movement in their confines. Consider shelter animals that are caged in tiny quarters with minimal contact or attention.

Nobody that I know wants to lose their driver's license. They want the sense of security that comes from being fully in charge of their movement at all times. Some drivers even seem to resent safety restraints behind the wheel or the traffic around them. They lock all doors upon entering their car, just as they lock all exterior and interior doors at home and put security locks on everything they own, including information and access. We like to be in control and stay inside our comfort lanes.

But the kind of deep, active meditation that we are going to use in programming a lucid dream requires the physical side of you to relinquish control, so that your physical brain and the rest of your body goes into a total rest phase. This goes against everything that some people fight to prevent. We see people who are asked to meditate, keeping one eye open and their consciousness humming, as every fiber of their physical bodies is keenly alert during their so-called meditation.

I have worked with students who insisted that their early meditation instructor assured them it was okay to remain a little in the physical world, with their senses awake, during a meditation. They have been assured that everyone who meditates stays a little bit connected to physical stimulation all around them.

By contrast, I try to demonstrate how a Samadhi mystic would approach meditation. Samadhi mystics follow the wisdom tradition of raja-yoga, or the yoga of higher consciousness. When one of them enters meditation, they completely turn off the physical world around them. They are oblivious to outside and internal sounds or any distractions. They are totally committed to entering a meditative state that is divorced from the physical world.

An example of how well even young Samadhi students engage themselves fully in a meditation comes from a recent storm. A major earthquake and subsequent tsunami in the Indian Ocean devastated Indonesia and the southern tip of India in 2004. Masters who were watching young novices in lucid dreaming wondered how they should deal with students who were deep in meditation during the storm. These students were oblivious to their surroundings, as they journeyed outside normal time and space for a prolonged period. The masters gently moved their sleeping bodies during the storm. None of the students came out of their meditations during the move. Some spent up to three days in their deep out-of-body dreams.

This is not unlike shamans who go into deep trances to leave their bodies during dream walking or spirit walking. They are oblivious to the physical world around them or the typical sensations of their physical bodies.

So how do they enter such a deep meditation or trance? Some people claim to learn to meditate by staring at a dot on the wall, gazing at a spiral that spins before their eyes, or listening to a bell or some other sound that is supposed to somehow trigger a departure into a meditative state. None of those gimmicks really work well, since they all engage the senses and the physical brain. The goal is to fully put the physical body, including the physical mind, to complete rest. These little tricks to hypnotize you into thinking that you are entering heightened consciousness and tuning out your physical presence might work for some low level of mediation or guided hypnosis. But we are not talking here about some quiet rest period or state of peaceful introspection. We are talking about leaving this world behind.

Entering a Deeper Meditation

Where your higher consciousness wants to take your inner spirit outside normal space and time requires a complete disconnect of your physical self. There can be no active physical activity such as idle thoughts or sensory awareness during this period, so that the body rests peacefully without function except necessary anatomical functions, such as breathing. There can be no trace of a signal that is operating within the body, including the mind.

In the material world, most people leave appliances plugged into power sockets even when the appliances are not in use. Consequently, there is always a little trickle of charge or connection going into the appliances. That includes a television, which ceases to show a picture or broadcast sound, even though it is still plugged into an electric outlet. To completely unplug a television so that no electrical power is attached, you can reach behind the appliance and disconnect the service cord that connects it to the wall socket. And that is sort of what we suggest that a person who is approaching a meditative state for lucid dreaming should do. Completely pull the plug on all power connections so that everything fades to black, with no signal or even a trickle coming through. Then you will see an emptiness inside you and complete stillness. In that vacuum, the spirit inside you can accelerate the intelligent energy that we call heightened consciousness. From that darkness comes new light. Then consciousness can take you on an amazing voyage of discovery outside the body and outside normal time and space.

There are various other altered states of consciousness one might enter for various reasons, but the depth of programming for a lucid dream requires special discipline to go further in totally numbing the body to enter a still point deep within you. That is where your inner self resides, and it needs room to maneuver without distraction.

Wholeness and Unity

Eastern spiritual science, which has studied yoga states for years, seeks union as a high goal in meditation. It is not the only discipline that attempts to establish an altered consciousness in the body to enable us to attain new direction and insight, but it is an ancient discipline that provides training and scope. Yoga seeks to align personal human consciousness to the divine as our spirit connects to universal spirit above us. Hence, union on a consciousness level as spirit is a goal in yoga in much the way that speaking to the spirit realm is the goal of the shaman.

To align our consciousness, then, we must reach harmony and unity within ourselves. This should not be an inner struggle but inner peace and accord. For many of us, sadly, wrestling with the intellect that is our analytical mind and its overload of sensual physical stimulation proves difficult. Even heroic Arjuna in the Hindu classic *The Bhagavad Gita: The Song of the Lord* finds the internal search of the soul challenging, despite having the lord by his side with sage advice. Here is what the lord told Arjuna:

> Knowing the soul to be superior to the material intellect, *subdue* the self (sense, mind, and intellect) by the self (strength of the soul). (BG 3:43)

So how do we subdue the mind to allow the soul that resides within us to surface? This is essential to any spiritual travelers, including lucid dreamers.

Note here that Lord Krishna or Krishna consciousness is NOT telling his spiritual student on his path of discovery to *slay* the mind, but to *subdue* it. Like Arjuna on the path, we can avoid internal conflict by simply coordinating elements within our whole being to allow time for our soul to come forward in our lives. So much of our internal concern, as ordinarily directed by our protective mind, is centered on survival, comfort, and control of our environment. But there comes an instance when these basic physical needs are met and greater concerns should be allowed to surface.

This can become an orderly and temporary transfer of responsibility. The physical mind and its sensory perception can be subdued with reason, since the physical mind considers itself the source of reason and is preoccupied with its ability to reason. Our mind will stand down for a short while once it is reasonably assured that it will be safe, rested, and unneeded for a limited duration that will not impair the body's overall condition. The mind, ever stressed day and night in trying to control everything about us, desperately wants and needs a time out. It simply becomes a matter of reasoning with our mind to shut down for good reason, allowing it only anatomical supervision of our basic physical life support during such adventures of the soul as lucid dreaming.

An Orderly Transfer of Directors

To reach such inner harmony, a lucid dreamer should spend some time at the outset to orchestrate this orderly transfer of power. The perfect occasion for bartering this peace would be just after the dreamer has carefully put the physical body to rest by focusing on the entire body from feet to head to direct it to become numb and lifeless. After doing that, the dreamer can logically begin deep, rhythmic breathing to energize the spirit within, then tune out all internal and external distractions that might otherwise occupy the protective mind. Once quieted and rested, the physical mind can be subdued.

You can access your heightened consciousness and the spirit within you once the body has become still and energized breathing calls the spirit forward. That presents the perfect opportunity to subdue the mind by bargaining with it to establish internal harmony. At this point, you can assure the mind that it is safe and can shut down, with the assurance that it will be rested and wonderfully restored in the process. It needs the assurance that the body will remain protected and safe. It also needs the assurance that control will be restored to the mind in short order. It needs to know that you will be okay and can safely slip out and slip back from your self-directed lucid dream outside time and space.

Once the mind has been rationally assured that the wholeness of your being will be safe during physical rest, it will be ready to relinquish control to your higher consciousness. The mind cannot rest during internal arguments, immediate safety matters, or potential worries. But it really harbors these overriding concerns only within the domain that it knows—your physical self and all its emotional and mental baggage of a mundane, basic nature. It has only vague understanding of subtle energy bodies, spirits, souls, and higher consciousness, which are nonphysical aspects of our whole being as pure energy.

Admit it: Your analytical brain has a difficult time in attempts to fully conceptualize subtle energy bodies, spirits, souls, and intelligent energy as inner consciousness. You might try to think about such things, but our mind is always dependent on seeing, measuring, and controlling things around in its sphere. By default, we accept what we cannot see or measure within us as moving parts of our reality, and we rely upon a sixth sense above our five physical levels of perception to recognize these energy aspects of our being. Our spirit innately knows that they are there, and knows what they do.

When we have reached the still point deep within us, we have probed beneath the surface of our superficial physical reality of reflections to the inner core, where spirit resides. I am reminded of a potter's wheel, where the artist works the surface of a glob of clay. At the center of all that clay on the wheel, however, we find the still point. This is the true hub of the project. This is the core of the entire project and anchors what shape it will become when carefully handled.

To reach a point when our spirit can leave the body freely in a self-directed lucid dream, we must reach the still point deep within us where there is total peace, tranquility, and inner joy for what lies ahead. Before that point, however, harmony and wholeness must be sensed throughout our entire being, with our mind as gatekeeper assured that our inner spirit can safely leave to safely return on cue.

There is nothing in a self-programmed lucid dream that is dangerous, risky, or unpredictable. While it is the ultimate adventure beyond normal space and time, it is controlled by careful planning and the assurance that you will fully return intact for a resumption of normal, physical activities.

Establishing a safe and protected place for your physical body to recline during lucid dreaming will add to the comfort and assurance of your mind that all will be well.

CHAPTER 8
Mapping Your Destination through Visualization

I have most always found success with individuals and groups in programming lucid dreams with focused visualization. In fact, that is the only sure way I have found for reaching a heightened state of altered awareness. This approach becomes even more valuable when we are attempting to program out-of-body experiences outside normal time and space.

Reaching an altered state of heightened consciousness is one of two main ways that I outlined planning a time shift to explore time travel in a previous book, *Time Shifts* (Destiny, 2021). The other approach, perhaps more familiar to many people, is to enter a conscious state of heightened awareness through meditation, which is covered in this guide as a programmed waking dream. Viewing this effort as a meditation is certainly more familiar to people familiar with Hindu yoga or Buddhist techniques. Meditation is simply an exercise to reach a goal. For many people, the goal of meditation seems superficial, depending on its depth.

I am choosing here to outline a programmed lucid dream as an approach to enable time travel, since dreams are familiar to everyone and lack certain religious scrutiny that sometimes is attached to meditation. Also, I wanted to avoid a common misconception of superficial navel gazing that unfortunately is associated with the ancient and important technique of meditation. I have tried to advocate meditation techniques elsewhere and fully appreciate the value of reaching meditative states, particularly with raja-yoga or so-called wisdom yoga, which seeks to tap and explore consciousness.

Since dreams can be programmed in the same way, meditation can be programmed internally, I have outlined step-by-step procedures for individuals to plan their own lucid dreams outside time and space in precisely the same way it can be done in meditation. While I have directed the steps here, I hasten to point out that the overarching expectation is for readers to discover how to self-direct their own lucid dreams. This includes harmonically tuning the wholeness of your being to allow the physical body and mind to fade into a rest cycle, activating higher consciousness to release the spirit within you, and then mapping the lucid dream specifically by drafting a diagram of where you want to go, what you want to experience, and what you intend to learn.

Drafting that diagram, which becomes your perfect map when you leave the body, will involve creative visualization. You might think of creative visualization with a simple formula: *thought, action, deed*. The process begins with a thought or concept. Then it is propelled by you as placing it into motion as a serious desire. It becomes a reality as you propel your focused desire into motion, marking the accomplishment as a deed. You might call this imaginative thinking. Noted Hawaiian shaman and author Serge Kahili King has called it *imagineering*, a term that describes how we can effectively engineer changes through the real powers that are often viewed as imagination (see *Imagineering for Health* [Hunaworks, 2014]). If you can see it, this approach suggests, then you can achieve it. Our key in creative visualization, then, involves our ability to see with new eyes.

Seeing with New Eyes, Hearing with New Ears

Many mystical directions encourage us to see with new eyes and develop deeper insight so that we can extend our vision beyond the limitations of our physical eyes. Many philosophers and spiritual teachers have advocated this quest. The Christian Bible is filled with this very directive throughout both the New and Old Testaments.

Great teachers and masters have long admonished their seekers to learn to see better, hear better, and knock to open doors of understanding, as I outlined in *Mysterious Messages from Beyond* (REDFeather, 2021). Now, you might be thinking that every healthy person has the ability to see, listen, and ask questions, right? But great masters ask more of their students than idle listening and glancing eyes. They ask their students to reach beyond the five perceptive senses we experience in the ordinary, physical world to gain a deeper insight into universal intelligence.

Jesus Christ challenged his disciples to see deeper and rebuked them for their lack of discernment. "Having eyes, see ye not, and having ears, hear ye not?" he told his disciples in Mark 8:18 in the King James Version (KJV) of the Holy Bible.

In Matthew 13–9 and 13–11 of the Bible, we read how Christ ended all seven letters to the church in Revelation with a similar challenge: "He that hath an ear, let him hear," the master said, referring to those who were "to know the mysteries of the kingdom of heaven."

Similarly, we see that Revelation 3:6 refers to ears to "hear what the Spirit saith." Hebrews 4:7 also challenges people to learn to "hear His voice."

How can we become discerning in this way? How can we improve our vision and learn to hear better? It almost seems like a hopeless task, perhaps—something only the shrewd can pick up. Actually, discernment isn't that hard if we focus. Discernment is simply acute awareness with the ability to understand. Lack of discernment, by contrast, shows a lack of refinement, cultivation, sophistication, sensitivity, and enlightenment. Lack of discernment indicates an inability to discriminate what is important from what is not.

Now, possibly you are still thinking that everyone, on the basis of experience, can listen carefully with their physical ears and see everything important around them with their eyes to discern what is important, right? But what if there is a deeper level of perception involved here, a level beyond the five perceptive senses of our ordinary, physical experience? Perhaps we are looking deeper for a heightened sense of awareness that goes beyond our five senses and the ordinary, physical world. After all, that is where masters usually direct us to seek deeper truth.

Krishnamurti and Castaneda

Indian sage Jiddu Krishnamurti, author of *At the Feet of the Master*, had much to say about developing discernment. Later, he built on his advice. "You as individuals have to comprehend the process of consciousness through direct, choiceless discernment," Krishnamurti said in 1936 during lectures in Ommen, Holland. "So, there must be deep, choiceless perception to comprehend the process of consciousness," he added. "If there is no discernment of the process of individual consciousness, then action will ever create confusion." Krishnamurti noted that "this great discernment of choiceless life implies great alertness."

The Mexican American anthropologist Carlos Castaneda wrote several books on the development of a heightened sense of awareness by learning to see without eyes and hear without ears, in what he described as "non-ordinary reality." His teachers encouraged him to open up on a deeper level of consciousness to see the unseen world all around us.

Lest anyone dismiss the books of Castaneda as fantasy or total fiction, consider that his first book was a project for his doctorate degree in anthropology from the University of California. *The Teachings of Don Juan: A Yaqui Way of Knowledge* and other books by the young anthropologist describe his shamanic training by Mexicans who traced their ancient Toltec roots in mysticism.

In book after book, on the basis of notes that Castaneda claimed he kept during his instruction, his mystic teachers encouraged him to see not with his physical eyes, but with a greater awareness, and to learn to listen with a sense of heightened consciousness to a world outside our normal senses that most people do not hear or see for lack of training.

Concern for this lack of seeing and hearing on a deeper level to reach inner hidden truth is apparent through the Christian Bible. Biblical references to ears that do not hear and eyes that do not see precede even the recorded teachings of Jesus, with many such references found in the Old Testament. In Deuteronomy 29:4, it is written, "Yet the Lord hath not given you a heart to perceive, and eyes to see, and ears to hear unto this day."

In Jeremiah 5:21, it is written, "Hear now this, O foolish people, and without understanding; which have eyes, and see not; which have ears, and hear not."

Similarly, we see in Ezekiel 12:2: "Son of man, thou dwell in the midst of a rebellious house, which have eyes to see, and see not; they have ears to hear, and hear not."

Isaiah 42:18–20 says, "Hear, ye deaf; and look, ye blind, that ye may see. . . . Seeing many things, but thou observest not; opening the ears, but he heareth not." And Isaiah 44:18 continues this point: "They have not known nor understood: for he hath shut their eye, that they cannot see; and their hearts, that they cannot understand."

In Psalms 69:23, it says, "Let their eyes be darkened, that they see not." And in Psalms 115:5, it is written, "They have mouths, but they speak not; eyes have they, but they see not. They have ears, but they hear not."

The New Testament of the Bible contains many such references to deeper seeing and deeper listening. Mark 4:12 says, "That seeing they may see, and not perceive; and hearing they may hear, and not understand." John 12:40 says, "He hath blinded their eyes, and hardened their hearts, that they should not see with their eyes."

Apparently, people have been born somewhat deaf and blind for many years. In Romans 11:8, it is written, "God hath given them the spirit of slumber, eyes that they should not see, and ears that they should not hear."

A lot of us seem to be asleep and missing a lot of important things being said and otherwise communicated. I have outlined the possibilities of what we are missing in *Mysterious Messages from Beyond* (REDFeather, 2021). Just who could be speaking to us? What are these unheard messages from beyond the pale? Likely, it could be divine voices, possibly the voice of God, angels, guides, nature spirits, or devas. It could be voices from the grave or other realms of the spirit world. It could be people you know who are desperately trying to reach you with information that they consider vital. It could be your lost pet. It could be voices from the past or the future. The possibilities are vast in a cosmos as large as ours, with worlds within worlds and endless skies before us. The question, always, is whether we are listening and attentive.

The young Indian sage J. Krishnamurti dedicated his early classic, *At the Feet of the Master*, to "Those Who Knock." Indeed, the seeker needs to indicate a receptivity for knowledge, a desire to hear deeper truths that might be revealed to those who are ready. And as the Indian sage acknowledges in his little classic, the seeker might just as easily be Buddhist, Hindu, Muslim, Jew, Jain, or Christian. Truth is truth to whoever knocks on the door and listens in earnest.

"Knock, and it shall be opened unto you," reads Luke 11:5 in the KJV of the Bible. "For everyone that asketh receiveth," it continues, "and he that seeketh findeth; and to him that knocketh it shall be opened."

Similarly, Matthew 7:7 of the KJV of the Bible states, "Ask, and it shall be given you; seek, and yet shall find; knock, and it shall be opened unto you."

When we seek to look beyond the limited surface of our physical world, where everything we see is simply a reflection of the light energy that has reflected off it, we realize deep down inside us that we need new eyes to see a nonphysical reality, and we need to open new doors through a heightened consciousness that is not limited to a three-dimensional world perceived only through five physical senses.

When we agree internally to put the physical senses and mental analysis of our body to rest, we climb beyond the gatekeeper that restricts what we can see, hear, and touch to a deeper reservoir of acute awareness. That awareness defines our heightened consciousness when the intelligent energy dwells deep within us as our eternal life force and spirit springs forward to spread its wings. When it unfolds itself, we experience a heightened sense of seeing, hearing, and feeling.

This is the acute awareness that allows us to visualize where we want to go, what we want to experience, and exactly what we seek to learn in our lucid dreams of self-discovery. This includes our inner eye, which allows us to draw a map of where we want to go. This includes how we knock on a new door of discovery in visualizing the map on which we draw our plans. This includes the focused intent of our inner spirit's deepest desire to explore, discover, and grow in understanding of who we are and our place in the grand plan.

We design our destiny when we visualize our map of where we intend to go in our lucid dream. The dreamscape brings us a little closer every time to realizing the full intent of our destiny. An expression I have always liked and find most appropriate here is this: "If you can see it, you can be it." In other words, we are visualizing our own reality and then realizing it as already manifest and formed.

Of course, that requires great desire, strength of will, and belief in ourselves. It recognizes that on a causal level of our being, we have the innate ability and energy to shape our desire with focused intent and cause change. Our causal body is all about intuition and the full range of what we can intuit. To activate this level of my own being, I always dig deep into my third chakra, which is often associated with the spleen or the solar plexus area of my body, and focus on swirling energetic properties of the color yellow, which is associated with this chakra.

The chakra, as an energy vortex, of course, is located on all subtle energy levels of our being, so it is not limited to this physical location. It is important to focus, however, on the power of the will that is magnetically energized by this key chakra and its impact on our overall mental energy. The soft pastel-yellow color associated with this energy center favorably impacts our confidence, emotional power, persuasion, and intense thought.

You also could make the connection to this chakra by focusing on the musical note E, which corresponds energetically to yellow in terms of energy vibrational patterns.

Now, these connections might seem like a lot to include in forming your creative visualization. We are suggesting that you focus on things such as the causal body, the third chakra, the color yellow, and the musical note E. You really do not need to include all of that in the beginning to simplify things, however. You could add these boosters to your visualization process as you continue setting up your lucid-dream visualizations. While tapping into these subtle energy levels will help you form a powerful visualization to take you where you want to go in your dreams, you can rest assured that they can function quite normally on your behalf automatically.

And if it seems as though the steps to creative visualization in mapping your lucid dream take too long at first, rest assured that time is not important here. You will be entering timelessness soon in your lucid dream, where time ceases to have any linear meaning whatsoever. And once at your dreamscape, time will pass very differently than in your physical experience. So forget about lost time and simply focus on the steps, since you will find it worthwhile to set up your lucid dream carefully to reach your goals.

Consequently, you should stop and begin the steps again if you sense that you are still half in the physical realm of sensation and thought and only halfway entering higher consciousness. Spirit will wait until you are ready to depart. There is no need to rush or plunge ahead if you are not fully engaged on a higher consciousness level.

Forming the Picture

We want to form a picture of where we want to go, what we want to explore, and what we intend to learn on the blank screen before our mind's eye. Forming a picture prevents us from resorting to words and thoughts that will engage our analytical mind. Make certain you wait for spirit to include any agenda that it has in mind. Deep inside, you innately know what journey you need to take.

Do not worry if the picture that forms on your blank screen seems sketchy. This is your personal map that will take you with unerring accuracy to the location you identify on the blank screen. Intuitively, you will know how to get there, and spirit will transcend the physical restraints of this material world to travel through time and space to wherever you need to go.

The map you create might include persons or pets you want to see, different times along the fluid timeline, events you want to review, and situations you want to study. You also might include what you would hope to learn, since your journey is a journey of self-discovery.

Not enough can be said of the value in previsualizing what and where you intend to go to focus your lucid-dream adventure. Creative visualization involves our higher thought forms and the thought power of the highest level of consciousness. It employs intelligent energy to direct our efforts to transcend here and now.

If you notice that the map you intend to draw on your blank slate seems slow to fill and has many gaps, ease up and let spirit lead the way. Allow spirit to draw the map for you. Simply study whatever appears on the slate before your mind's eye. Always remember that spirit knows your origins, knows the life mission that you are trying to rediscover, and knows what the future holds for you. Spirit is always there at all stages of your eternal life and can fill in any gaps that might confuse you during this particular lifetime.

Visualizing a Dream Guide

There is truly little you cannot visualize and manifest in your life if you follow the steps for creative visualization and project your energized thought forms with focused intent. You can even manifest a dream guide to assist you in your lucid dreaming beyond space and time, where few of us have a recognized sense of reference or confidence to approach.

I almost hesitate to raise the possibility of manifesting a guide, since the primary focus in this book is to assure you that you alone can self-direct your lucid dreams to plan and execute with smooth, personal departures to the dreamscape of your choosing. After all, this is your journey of self-discovery, and nobody can effectively direct you better than you can yourself. You know internally exactly what you need to experience and learn in these life adventures in an altered state of consciousness.

On the other hand, a dream guide can offer support to you in your initial dreamwork if you have concerns in the beginning. I can certainly relate to those concerns, since initially I tried lucid dreaming on my own, without any advance information to guide me. In fact, I stumbled into it one night, as many of you might have done in unplanned, random vivid dreams. My first experience with lucid dreaming came as an accident when I fell on my lower back and somehow triggered an out-of-body lucid dream, which happened decades ago when I lived on Mount Hood in Oregon. I described my experiences in an earlier book, *Conversations with the Dream Mentor: Awaken to Your Inner Guide* (Llewellyn, 2003).

I recognize now that I am hardly the only person who has worked with a dream guide. At the time, however, I thought I had practically invented the process of manifesting a guide for my dreams. I had previous knowledge, however, from an earlier account of working with a dream guide from the book *Dream Master* by Eckankar master Harold Klemp (who coincidentally hails from my own hometown of Everett, Washington).

In the beginning, it seemed that I had magically summoned a guide to assist me. Looking back now, I can see that I actually manifested this guide through creative visualization. It appears that the potential to bring a guide into our lives is completely within our innate ability to conceive, achieve, and believe a thought form that we have empowered with focused intent to become part of our moving reality. Anyone can do it with the sort of simple creative visualization that we have discussed here. In fact, you can visualize helpers to assist you in many phases of your life and manifest people and events that you visualize with the power of your active thought forms if you truly desire and need them. The approach is always the same, as the book *Manifesting* (REDFeather, 2021) outlines.

In the case of manifesting my own dream guide, I worried that my initial ventures into lucid dreams could be awkward and even dangerous. I had no guidance or confidence. Consequently, I fretted that I would leave my body and not be able to negotiate my way beyond my cabin in the woods and might even get lost in the great beyond. I worried that I would get into trouble if I ventured too far from my physical body. I even worried that I might have difficulty returning safely and efficiently to my body.

And my initial experiences in leaving my body in a lucid dream did seem rather clunky to me, but that was simply due to the way I chose to view it. I recall rising up in the room above my body and lifting beyond the roof of my cabin in the woods. I recall moving higher above the tall Douglas fir trees that surrounded the house, and sensing the night sky. The sky seemed immense and something that I could drown in. That is simply the way I chose to see it.

None of those physical concerns are real, however, in a state of heightened consciousness when your spirit leaves the physical body. You can be assured that you will be safe and move freely outside normal time and space when you leave your physical body in a lucid dream. The spirit that dwells within us knows where it needs to go and how to get there. Your map directs it on its way. Your consciousness reaches its goal effortlessly, like an arrow to its certain target. While the physical self might get lost in the physical world, time and again, your spirit innately knows how to negotiate the nonphysical realm outside mundane space and time. And when this traveling spirit is ready to return to your physical body, safely resting in a room far away, it will instantly return to your sleeping self. It will return because it has found what it set out to find in the dreamscape. It will return to your physical self like two ends of a magnet that cannot be separated long, connected by karmic attraction. This is electromagnetic energy at work.

I visualized the sort of guide that I thought might assist me in my dreams, and in short order she did materialize in my lucid dream, ready to grasp my hand and pull me beyond those tall fir trees in the dark sky above my cabin. She was exactly the way I pictured her, and became more and more defined the longer I knew her.

My guide, Selina, eventually got me over my initial concerns as she escorted me on various lucid dreams of intense discovery. She assured me that I could visualize where I wanted to go. I would instantly find myself there without all the drama of floating through treelines in a dense night sky. As I continued to meet Selina in my lucid dreams, she began to suggest things to explore in these dreams. The decision was always mine, although she did not always agree with my decision, often voicing strong concerns over my daring choices.

After several lucid-dream journeys together, Selina gave me a test to see whether she should continue as my guide. When I failed her test, she handed me off to another dream guide, someone she considered her master. And I never saw Selina again in a dreamscape, although I did occasionally catch a sideways glance of her watching me. Instead, my lucid dreams were assisted for a time by an elderly man who always met me on a shore in my lucid dreams to begin each lesson.

In time, this dream guide no longer appeared to me, and I did not manifest him. I had learned with the assistance of my dream guides to direct and execute my own voyages of discovery.

CHAPTER 9
Step-by-Step Setup for the Dreamscape

While we have outlined in earlier chapters how to effectively prepare yourself for a self-directed lucid dream with creative visualization and a heightened state of consciousness, some exercises that show how to do this step by step might make it easier for you. Once again, please do not consider this to be outside guidance, but only suggestions on how to program your own lucid dreams on a personal level. These sort of lucid dreams of discovery and insight are purely of your own design. This is your own arc of a hero's journey, and a solo adventure with meaning meant only for you. Consequently, it is best that you try to study these exercises thoroughly in advance so that you can do them on your own without an outside guide or assistant. You do not want to try doing these exercises with the book in one hand for reference or always turning back to the book for guidance. You should be able to internalize the message after reading over one of the exercises carefully several times. An option would be to record your own voice reading the step-by-step instructions. While you should try to do this on your own, it would not be bad to have a helper across the room who is softly reading the instructions to you in the beginning.

The first two exercises will take you through mapping without manifesting a dream guide, while the last two exercises will show how to work with a guide if desired. The initial exercise will include steps to fill out your own map and depart the physical body, while the second exercise will show how to patiently wait until spirit fills out the agenda on your blank slate. The third exercise will show how to set your agenda and then manifest a guide to assist you on your dreamscape. The last exercise will show how to manifest a guide to direct you on your dreamscape outside time and space, without a personal agenda. That will give you options, so that you can find a comfort level of your own choosing in setting up your own lucid dreams.

EXERCISE 1

Preparing a Map to Leave the Body outside Time and Space

NEEDED:

- quiet, secluded place where you can recline peacefully without interruption
- bed or floor mat to recline on your back (preferred), or else a straight-back chair to sit on
- loose-fitting clothing, with shoes, socks, and any jewelry or watch removed
- interior lighting preferably turned off, although natural light from a window helps

Initial Procedure

1. Recline on your back with arms and legs outstretched at 45-degree angles, or sit erect with feet firmly grounded if you choose to sit in a chair. Do not cross any fingers or legs, so that energy can flow freely within you.
2. Focus your attention on putting the physical body to sleep, beginning with the feet and working upward to the head.
3. Begin deep, rhythmic breathing and continue until it becomes regular.
4. Tune out all internal and external distractions until you become still and quiet inside yourself.
5. Once you become comfortable and feel that you have reached an inner peace, assure your physical mind that it can go into a deep sleep mode with the rest of your body for a short while, allowing your heightened consciousness to come forward.

Preparing a Map

1. Notice that your heightened consciousness is now racing, while your body and analytical mind rests.
2. You will see a darkness inside yourself. In that darkness, project a clear blank slate in front of your mind's eye.
3. Begin to draw a picture of a time and place that you want to visit in your dreamscape and what characters and lessons you wish to discover there. Do not think in words or sounds, but only in pictures. Do not analyze your pictures. Your consciousness will understand them and accept them as a clear map to take you where you want to go.

4. Sense your causal body with its intuitive abilities, and sense the chakra power of your will center to power you in your journey outside the physical body. (You might see the yellow or orange-yellow light energy or hear the musical note E inside you without uttering a sound. Rely on your acute awareness.)
5. Now tuck the map you have drawn into the back of your consciousness, recognizing that when you recall it, you will automatically leave your physical body, with this map as your perfect guide.
6. Reconcile yourself to leaving your physical body in your journey, then recall the map to trigger your automatic departure beyond known space and time.

At the Dreamscape

1. When you arrive at your dreamscape, orient yourself to your presence there and your surroundings. You will notice that you do not have your physical body or common sensory perception, but a subtle body with new powers of awareness. Assure yourself that you are present and experiencing things there with acute awareness with new eyes.
2. Carefully observe without personal involvement. Become the perfect witness without interaction.
3. There are various things in your mapping that you intended to encounter, observe, and learn in this lucid dream. Patiently wait for everything to evolve before you.
4. When you sense completion in the sense that you have seen and attempted to learn everything you intended, then return your focus back to your physical body in the room where it is resting.
5. You should find yourself instantly back in your physical body.
6. When you return to your physical body, slowly allow yourself to adjust to your physical presence and the room around you.
7. Stay in a conscious state to meditate on your lucid-dream experience with eyes closed, simply picturing all that you have observed, without analysis.
8. After capturing the dream memories, allow yourself to return sensation to your physical body.
9. Slowly open your eyes as the physical mind returns from its deep sleep.
10. Take your time gently getting to your feet.
11. You might quietly sit to jot down your memories in a dream journal, without attempting to analyze them.

Postscript

1. You can return to the same dreamscape over and over until you have fully absorbed the lessons there and satisfied yourself. Simply map the same time and place on your blank slate with the objectives that concern you.
2. As you see a pattern and the pattern becomes clearer to you with each journey of self-discovery, you can begin to try to process your lucid dreams. Recognize that they will mean more to you on a spirit level than a physical level that could be processed analytically by your mind.

EXERCISE 2
Letting Spirit Fill Out Your Dance Card

(Note: This and subsequent exercises are similar to the prior exercise, with some variations.)

NEEDED:

- quiet, secluded place where you can recline peacefully without interruption
- bed or floor mat so you can recline on you back (preferred), or else a straight-back chair to sit on
- loose-fitting clothing, with shoes, socks, and any jewelry or watch removed
- interior lighting preferably turned off, although natural light from a window helps

Initial Procedure

1. Recline on your back, with arms and legs outstretched at 45-degree angles, or sit erect with feet firmly grounded if you choose to sit in a chair. Do not cross any fingers or legs, so that energy can flow freely within you.
2. Focus your attention on putting the physical body to sleep, beginning with the feet and working upward to the head.
3. Begin deep, rhythmic breathing and continue until it becomes regular.
4. Tune out all internal and external distractions until you become still and quiet inside yourself.
5. Once you become comfortable and feel that you have reached an inner peace, assure your physical mind that it can go into a deep sleep mode with the rest of your body for a short while, allowing your heightened consciousness to come forward.

Preparing a Map

1. In the prior exercise, notice that your heightened consciousness is now racing, while your body and analytical mind rests.
2. Look deeply into yourself with your mind's eye, without thought or analysis, and see a clean, blank slate before you.
3. Ask your internal spirit to fill the slate for you, drawing a map of where you need to go and what you need to see. It may include characters that you need to study there and an event that you need to witness. It might include what you need to learn in this dreamscape.
4. Now patiently wait for spirit to fill out your blank slate to provide you with everything that you will need to observe in your lucid dream. Simply focus on the slate without analyzing it. You will be able to understand the chart and use it as an unerring map to take your consciousness wherever and whenever it needs to go for your observation.
5. Sense your causal body with its intuitive abilities, and sense the chakra power of your will center to power you in your journey outside the physical body. (You can see the yellow or orange-yellow light energy and hear the musical note E inside you without uttering a sound. Use your acute awareness.)
6. Now tuck the map that spirit has drawn for you into the back of your consciousness, recognizing that when you recall it, you will automatically leave your physical body, with this map as your perfect guide.
7. Reconcile yourself to leaving your physical body in your journey, then recall the map to trigger your departure outside space and time.

At the Dreamscape

1. When you arrive at this dreamscape, orient yourself to your presence there and your surroundings. You will notice that you do not have your physical body or common sensory perception, but a subtle body with new powers of awareness. Assure yourself that you are present and experiencing things there with acute awareness with new eyes.
2. Carefully observe without personal involvement. Become the perfect witness without interaction.
3. There are various things in your mapping that you intended to encounter, observe, and learn in this lucid dream. Patiently wait for everything to evolve before you.
4. When you sense completion in the sense that you have seen and learned everything you intended, then return your focus back to your physical body in the room where it is resting.

5. You should find yourself instantly back in your physical body.
6. When you return to your physical body, slowly allow yourself to adjust to your physical presence and the room around you.
7. Stay in a conscious state to meditate on your lucid-dream experience, simply picturing all that you have observed, without analysis.
8. After capturing the dream memories, allow yourself to return sensation to your physical body.
9. Slowly open your eyes as the physical mind returns from its deep sleep.
10. Take your time gently getting to your feet.
11. You might quietly sit to jot down your memories in a dream journal, without attempting to analyze them at this point.

Postscript

1. You can return to the same dreamscape over and over until you have fully absorbed the messages there and satisfied yourself. Simply map the same time and place on your blank slate with the objectives that concern you.
2. As you see a pattern and it becomes clearer to you with each journey of self-discovery, you can begin to try to analyze your lucid dreams. Recognize that they will mean more to you on a spirit level than a physical level that can be easily processed.

EXERCISE 3

Manifesting a Dream Guide after Setting Your Map Goals

(Note: This will be similar to earlier exercises, with variations.)

NEEDED:
- quiet, secluded place where you can recline peacefully without interruption
- bed or floor mat so you can recline on you back (preferred), or else a straight-back chair to sit on
- loose-fitting clothing, with shoes, socks, and any jewelry or watch removed
- interior lighting preferably turned off, although natural light from a window helps

Initial Procedure

1. Recline on your back, with arms and legs outstretched at 45-degree angles, or sit erect with feet firmly grounded if you choose to sit in a chair. Do not cross any fingers or legs, so that energy can flow freely within you.
2. Focus your attention on putting the physical body to sleep, beginning with the feet and working upward to the head.
3. Begin deep, rhythmic breathing and continue until it becomes regular.
4. Tune out all internal and external distractions until you become still and quiet inside yourself.
5. Once you become comfortable and feel that you have reached an inner peace, assure your physical mind that it can go into a deep sleep mode with the rest of your body for a short while, allowing your heightened consciousness to come forward.

Preparing a Map

1. Notice that your heightened consciousness is now racing, while your body and analytical mind rests.
2. In the dark void, project a blank tablet or slate before your mind's eye.
3. Begin to draw a picture of the time and place that you want to visit in your dreamscape and what characters and lessons you wish to discover there. Do not think in words or sounds, but only in pictures. Do not analyze your pictures. Your consciousness will understand them and accept them as a clear map to take you where you want to go.
4. Sense your causal body with its intuitive abilities, and sense the chakra power of your will center to power you in your journey outside the physical body. (You can see the yellow or orange-yellow light energy and hear the musical note E inside you without uttering a sound. Use your new sense of acute awareness for this.)
5. Now tuck the map you have drawn into the back of your consciousness, recognizing that when you recall it, you will automatically leave your physical body with this map.
6. Reconcile yourself to leaving your physical body in your journey, then recall the map.
7. Now visualize creating a dream guide to assist you. Draw a picture of this guide with your mind's eye on a new blank screen before you. Design how this guide will look and the guide's demeanor. Create the qualities in this guide that you believe will help you in your dream search. Be patient, since this creation might take awhile to visualize.

8. Now tuck that picture back into the back of your consciousness and recall your original map along with the dream guide that you have called to join you, with the assurance that when you do, you will be prepared to instantly leave on your journey with your guide.

At the Dreamscape

1. When you arrive at your dreamscape, orient yourself to your presence there and your surroundings. Observe your dream guide by your side. You will notice that you do not have your physical body or common sensory perception, but a subtle body with new powers of awareness. Assure yourself that you are present and experiencing things there with acute awareness with new eyes.
2. Carefully observe without personal involvement. Become the perfect witness without interaction.
3. There are various things in your mapping that you will need to encounter, observe, and learn in this lucid dream. Patiently wait for everything to evolve before you, and pay attention to any directions or clues from your guide.
4. When you sense completion in the sense that you have seen and learned everything that is important for you, return your focus back to your physical body in the room where it is resting.
5. You should find yourself instantly back in your physical body.

After Your Lucid Dream

1. When you return to your physical body, slowly allow yourself to adjust to your physical presence and the room around you.
2. Stay in a conscious state to meditate on your lucid-dream experience with eyes closed, simply picturing all that you have observed, without analysis.
3. After capturing the dream memories, allow yourself to return sensation to your physical body.
4. Slowly open your eyes as the physical mind returns from its deep sleep.
5. Take your time gently getting to your feet.
6. You might quietly sit to jot down your memories in a dream journal, without attempting to analyze them at this point.

Postscript

1. If you have trouble creating and traveling with a dream guide, you probably need to spend some extra time visualizing this mentor. You might try putting the physical body to sleep, entering controlled

breathing, and drawing a picture of your perfect dream guide on a clear blank slate, outside of any planned lucid dream at that time.
2. Dream guides, once visualized by the dreamer, will assume their own characteristics outside those that you have originally drawn for them. They will take on a life of their own as someone who knows precisely what you need to experience and how you need to experience it in a dreamscape. You are really connecting with a guide who fits your needs. Trust the guide, who is a supernatural being. Some people consider the guide to be our higher self or our guiding angel. Treat the guide with the utmost respect.

EXERCISE 4

Manifesting a Guide without a Personally Mapped Agenda

(Note: This will be somewhat similar to earlier exercises, with variations.)

NEEDED:

- quiet, secluded place where you can recline peacefully without interruption
- bed or floor mat so you can recline on you back (preferred), or else a straight-back chair to sit on
- loose-fitting clothing, with shoes, socks, and any jewelry or watch removed
- interior lighting preferably turned off, although natural light from a window helps

Initial Procedure

1. Recline on your back, with arms and legs outstretched at 45-degree angles, or sit erect with feet firmly grounded if you choose to sit in a chair. Do not cross any fingers or legs, so that energy can flow freely within you.
2. Focus your attention on putting the physical body to sleep, beginning with the feet and working upward to the head.
3. Begin deep, rhythmic breathing and continue until it becomes regular.
4. Tune out all internal and external distractions until you become still and quiet inside yourself.
5. Once you become comfortable and feel that you have reached an inner peace, assure your physical mind that it can go into a deep sleep mode with the rest of your body for a short while, allowing your heightened consciousness to come forward.

Preparing a Map

1. Notice that your heightened consciousness is now racing, while your body and analytical mind rests.
2. Look deeply into yourself with your mind's eye, without thought or analysis, and see a clean, blank slate before you.
3. Sense your causal body with its intuitive abilities, and sense the chakra power of your will center to power you in your journey outside the physical body. (You can see the yellow or orange-yellow light energy and hear the musical note E inside you without uttering a sound. Use your acute awareness.)
4. Reconcile yourself to leaving your physical body in your journey as soon as your map is prepared for you.
5. Now visualize creating a dream guide to assist you. Draw a picture of this guide with your mind's eye on a new blank screen before you. Design how this guide will look and the guide's demeanor. Create the qualities in this guide that you believe will help you in your dream search. Visualize this guide preparing your agenda of what you need to see and where you need to go in your dreamscape with your guide. Be patient, since this creation might take awhile to visualize.
6. Now tuck that picture back into the back of your consciousness and recall your picture of the dream guide that you have called to totally guide you, with the assurance that you will be prepared to instantly leave on your journey with your guide.

At the Dreamscape

1. When you arrive at your dreamscape, orient yourself to your presence there and your surroundings. Observe your dream guide by your side. You will notice that you do not have your physical body or common sensory perception, but a subtle body with new powers of awareness. Assure yourself that you are present and experiencing things there with acute awareness with new eyes.
2. Carefully observe without personal involvement. Become the perfect witness without interaction.
3. There are various things in your mapping that you intended to encounter, observe, and learn in this lucid dream. Patiently wait for everything to evolve before you, and pay attention to any directions or clues from your guide.

4. When you sense completion in the sense that you have seen and learned everything you intended, then return your focus back to your physical body in the room where it is resting.
5. You should find yourself instantly back in your physical body.

After Your Lucid Dream

1. When you return to your physical body, slowly allow yourself to adjust to your physical presence and the room around you.
2. Stay in a conscious state to meditate on your lucid-dream experience, simply picturing all that you have observed, without analysis.
3. After capturing the dream memories, allow yourself to return sensation to your physical body.
4. Slowly open your eyes as the physical mind returns from its deep sleep.
5. Take your time gently getting to your feet.
6. You might quietly sit to jot down your memories in a dream journal, without attempting to analyze them at this point.

Postscript

1. As you continue to practice lucid dreaming, it might become more common for you to allow your internal spirit to draw the plan for where and what you will experience in your vivid dreams of discovery. Similarly, it might become more comfortable for you to work with a dream guide, particularly in earlier stages of your lucid dreaming.
2. Many people continue this approach in their ongoing practice of programming their lucid dreams. Of course, you will begin to understand and reach a comfort level in your dreams outside normal time and space and might begin to draw your own maps and travel alone at some point. It will be totally up to you how you program your own dreams of discovery.

CHAPTER 10

What to Expect in the Lucid Dreamscape

Some people might expect that something unpredictable or unsettling awaits them in a dreamscape during a lucid dream. While that is possible, let me assure you that programming your own self-directed lucid dream with specific goals that you have mapped for your journey should take much of the guesswork out of the process. Then the adventure in an altered state of space and time assumes your own personal agenda that has been established in advance.

Of course, an accidental lucid dream that is not planned can prove unpredictable on one level. Only your inner spirit, which has launched you on an unprogrammed lucid dream of personal discovery, will have an idea in advance of what awaits you in your dreamscape.

Also, allowing your inner spirit to draw your map on the clear blank slate before your mind's eye (as described in exercise 2 of the last chapter) will give you only a little indication and warning of what awaits you in your lucid dream. You will be able to view the agenda that spirit has mapped for you before your mind's eye before departure, but it will be little warning and possibly a little unclear to you what spirit has prioritized for your learning dream.

Another possibility that might leave you uncertain about what to expect in your dream would be a dreamscape that is directed by a dream guide. If you allow your dream guide to set the agenda for you in your lucid dream, as described in exercise 4 in the last chapter, then you are surrendering control to a guide who can determine your dream mapping and what lessons await you at your dream destination.

In all totally self-directed lucid dreams, where you set your own dream agenda by drawing your dream goals on a blank slate before your mind's eye, you are completely aware before embarking on your dream exactly what awaits you. You can always take complete control of your lucid dream, planning when you leave and what you will experience. The choice is yours.

Let us consider the possible situations with regard to what you can expect in your lucid dream. We will first consider exercises whereby you concede some control to your inner spirit and a dream guide. In such instances, they might set the dream agenda for you.

What to Expect When You Ask Spirit to Plan

Let us first outline what awaits you when you allow the spirit that dwells within you to draft your agenda in a lucid dream. The first assurance you have in this scenario, of course, is that your inner spirit is not some outside, foreign agent that is alien to you and your deepest concerns. I recognize that many people might not be fully aware of this inner spirit and fear that it borders on some sort of spirit possession. That is hardly the case here.

Your inner spirit has always been with you as the most permanent and eternal aspect of your whole being. It is your hidden self, your true self in the sense that it is the part of you that is not part of the passing parade of transient matter you experience in your physical body. It is totally aware and concerned about your progress in the grand scheme of things through many lifetimes in many life situations in a changing world of material form.

As such, it will not throw you a dangerous curve. It knows where you have been in the distant past, knows the shortcomings that you experience in this current life, and remembers the life mission and purpose that launched you into this life experience, even though a superficial aspect of you on a physical level now has forgotten. It knows what you need to remember, learn, and internalize within the wholeness of your being to proceed toward your grand life mission. Consequently, it understands the arc of your own hero's journey more than any aspect of you. So, trust your inner spirit to guide you. Get out of the way of yourself to listen to your inner voice.

Whatever your inner spirit will draft for you as an agenda on your lucid dream will appear as a solid plan for you to review on the clear blank slate in front of your mind's eye before departure to your dreamscape. You can examine the goals drawn lovingly and knowingly by spirit on your blank slate as an unerring map to take you on a journey of certain discovery and personal insight. Trust yourself. The spirit that dwells within you as your eternal self knows you better than anyone and will direct you carefully.

This takes the guesswork out of planning a meaningful lucid dream. When spirit fills out your dance card, you only have to examine the beauty of the agenda to know you are in good hands. Otherwise, you could spend time drawing a plan that seems to draw upon your heightened consciousness in a process that involves your inner spirit but is not a direct process of letting spirit draw the plan effortlessly.

In this scenario, you simply wait with patience and confidence while spirit draws upon your clear blank slate as your map of discovery. When you arrive at your dreamscape destination, you will have seen the map before, leaving your physical body with the certainty that spirit is directing you.

What to Expect with a Dream Guide

There is a little less certainty when you rely totally on a dream guide to direct you where you go in a lucid dream. You will be trusting the dream guide to take you where and when you need to go, without a map that you have drawn on the clear blank slate before your mind's eye.

It is possible, of course, to draw your map with an agenda of everything you want to explore in your dreamscape and then have your dream guide assist you on your journey of discovery. There would be fewer surprises with that approach, since you have personally prioritized your agenda in the dream.

But this chapter will consider what happens when you allow your dream guide to take you on a lucid dream that you have not personally drawn, with confidence in the guide to show you what you really need to see and learn.

First, let us remember that the way you creatively visualize and manifest a dream guide ensures that you have brought the ideal escort and teacher to your side. This is your idealized vision of the perfect guide who will always act in your best interest. This visualized guide is an extension of you in a very real sense. It would be incorrect for you to fear or distrust anything about a guide that you have creatively visualized and manifested to help you in your dreamwork. This is not an outside entity that you have stumbled across, but a real part of you and your life.

I can tell you a little about my dream guides. The first, Selina, helped me in many ways since I manifested her. She helped me overcome my fear of traveling beyond normal space and time and held on to me securely, as I desired. As our adventures together continued, she began to choose the dreamscape I would visit with her. She determined the time and place of my dreams and what I would experience there, on the basis of what she thought I was ready to process. She challenged me more than I would have challenged myself at that point, but also tried to protect me from going places that I was not ready to experience. She cautioned me to avoid going too far beyond this earthly realm, as I began to develop a curiosity about other realms of reality.

Having read the first edition of Harold Klemp's book about a dream mentor and various higher spiritual realms that he visited with the guide, I wanted to explore the various levels of heavens myself. I never saw them as something that I was unready to explore, but my dream guide did. In fact, she refused to be a part of it. Standing in front of a god who sat enthroned before a river of light and claimed to be the master and creator of the world did prove frightening to me. I was not ready to see that or to proceed beyond a wooden bridge to the next level of heaven. Selina knew what was right for me and the sort of lessons that I was ready to internalize at that point of my spiritual travels in lucid dreams.

So she gave me a riddle to solve. She took me down a little animal trail in dense woods, as she often chose to do. When it forked into two separate paths, she pointed to an old, hollowed-out tree that loomed at that juncture. She continued to point high up the tall tree, where a bird emerged from a hole, perched on the edge, and then flew away. Selina asked me to tell her the significance of what I had been shown.

I tried many times to give her an answer that fully satisfied her. Sometimes she would smile with encouragement, somewhat pleased that I saw any significance in the bird-in-the-tree scenario. But ultimately, she determined that I had failed to solve what I now call "Selina's riddle."

When she determined that I could not fully appreciate the significance of what I had been shown on the trail in this lucid dream she programmed for me, she told me I was not ready to continue with her. Looking back, she had my best interest at heart, deciding that she couldn't help me at that point in my development.

But Selina did not abandon me. No, she introduced me to a wise guide that she claimed was her own teacher. She brought me to this man, whom I always found waiting for me beside the Aegean Sea. When the three of us were assembled at the shore on a sandy beach near the water's edge, Selina extended one arm toward the man and said, "This is my teacher. He will help you now." And then she vanished, never to visit or travel with me in my lucid dreams again. But the man in the white toga was a constant companion to me in future lucid dreams.

This squat, old man of my dreams would set the table for what I would see and experience in many future lucid dreams. He would walk with me in the shallow edge of the sea and show me how to see with new eyes, to experience the magic and impact of color and light as I had never envisioned before on my own. He taught me to see new color that I could not see before. He simply instructed me to scoop a bucket of stones under the water and cast them upon shore to display the energy of color inherent in these various stones. He taught me how to discern where electromagnetic stones of great potential, known as the philosopher's stone, were hidden in a collected pile of rocks. He took me into a dark-roofed cave, where I could not see anything, in an exercise to find the hidden light, acknowledging that light is always available to us if we can truly learn to see with new eyes.

In time, I learned many things with this new dream mentor and began to travel without him, strengthened by what he had taught me. I began to see the potential within myself to draw my own map with an agenda of what I now understood to be the lessons I needed to learn, trusting my own inner self to guide me. So, the lessons that Selina and the old man by the seaside had prepared me well for were my own voyages of discovery in future lucid dreams that I programmed on my own.

What to Expect with a Random Lucid Dream

A lucid dream that comes to you without any sort of planning is called into being by the spirit that dwells within you, with an agenda that is known only to your inner spirit. Since your inner spirit is an integral part of your whole being, the agenda and mapping of your dreamscape should not be jarring or terribly surprising to you. On a deep level, your consciousness will understand the selection of time, place, and circumstances for the lucid dream. It is precisely what your inner spirit knows you need.

Of course, this is not exactly like a planned lucid dream that you have visualized on a blank slate before your mind's eye with careful preparation to include every aspect of the dreamscape that you have in mind. That approach would give you more notice of where and when you plan your out-of-body voyage of discovery, as you ponder what you would like to observe and learn in the dream.

In such cases with advance dream planning, you will not find yourself suddenly at a dreamscape and trying to adapt to the time, place, and circumstances of the scene before you. Also, you would not need to spend much effort upon arrival, orienting yourself to your new dreamscape surroundings to determine that you are witnessing something that can be instructive but will not involve you in direct interaction.

So, there is much to say for the lucid dream that you totally plan in advance on your own, although a vivid dream that is directed by spirit or a guide can be profoundly rewarding and perhaps even more insightful, given the advanced awareness of your inner spirit and that of a dream guide.

The main thing to remember in any case is that there is no need for undue apprehension with any lucid dream in what you can expect when you find yourself at your dreamscape. You could be miles from home in an entirely different world or period of time, but that should not alarm you whatsoever. You will be perfectly safe in an out-of-body dream that is intended to gift you with insight that you could never find in your physical body during waking hours.

In terms of what you can expect when you arrive at your dreamscape, it really matters little whether you have totally programmed your own agenda and set your own map or had things arranged for you by your inner spirit or a dream guide. You will always be placed in the time, place, and circumstances that you most need to study and absorb to orient you to better understand where you have been and where you are going.

CHAPTER 11

Selecting Destinations Anywhere, Anytime

Because most people think of a dream in the common sense as creations of the restless mind during sleep, they do not believe that a dream can actually take them outside the physical body to virtually any time and any place that spirit longs to explore. But a lucid dream is much more than a limited bouncing around of internal memories inside our heads to resurface concerns of the past and future that our brains will not let rest.

As we have seen, a lucid dream is different, with no physical barriers or restrictions of the brain. It is not the cranking away at problems that cannot be easily resolved by the analytical mind, try as it will. It is limitless and boundless in its outbound journey of discovery and new insight.

And since the lucid dream occurs outside the physical realm as an exploration of conscious energy, it does not restrict our inner self or spirit to the material laws of physics with regard to time and space. Our spirit, then, transcends space-time in the physical sense and travels outside the physical body freely at the speed of light. There are literally no restrictions or filters that impede the free spirit from leaving the body to beyond what we normally consider here and now.

There are many implications to this new freedom, and they are profound and enlightening. You can go anywhere you can visualize to establish a conscious presence. Despite leaving your physical senses behind, you will be able to see, hear, touch, smell, and taste anything and everything you encounter in the dreamscape with new eyes and new ears that are associated with awareness of heightened awareness.

Not having physical legs to walk or fingers to touch does not restrict your ability to move about freely beyond the physical body and intimately examine everything around you in whatever time and place you choose for your dream adventure.

It is important, then, to truly believe when you enter a dreamscape during a lucid dream that you are actually present in consciousness and awareness and that everything you observe is just as real as the mundane physical world you left behind in your voyage of the spirit.

This is, of course, similar to how people in remote viewing are able to make such keen observations outside the physical body, and how their accurate accounts of what they observe are reliable and valuable.

Government, industry, and others rely on the acute awareness of remote viewing by people who leave their physical surroundings behind to roam and explore with their heightened consciousness. The value of what lucid dreamers discover and the extent to which they can explore is just as great, since the approach to programming a lucid dream is similar to the outward exploration in remote viewing.

To get a total picture of the extent to what we can explore and how far we can roam in lucid dreaming, we need to outline what it means to direct our heightened consciousness through space and time. Quite literally, there are no apparent limits. If you properly visualize and map a lucid dream to take you into the future or the past, you will instantly find yourself there. If you visualize and map a dreamscape that is far removed from your physical surroundings, you will find yourself in far regions of the world, on other worlds, or even in other realities outside the restrictions of our three-dimensional mundane existence.

How Far Can This Lucid Dream Take Me?

If you wonder how far you can roam outside your body in a lucid dream, you should next ask yourself where your inner spirit longs to go to explore. You are limited only by imagination and your innate ability to creatively visualize where you want to go. You can project yourself to the other side of the globe in a blink and return just as quickly by projecting your desire and power of your will to transport you. We are confined in a physical sense only by our ordinary focused intent on the space and time where we reside during the day. We are like gross beasts that walk the earth and stare at the ground in front of us as defining our presence in this limited way.

You could visualize and map your lucid dream to take you to the top of the tallest glacier or inside the deepest, darkest mine. You could visualize and project your consciousness to the middle of an ocean or on a mountaintop.

Moreover, you could visualize and project your consciousness to other worlds that most of us only gaze at in the distant skies. This is not simply imagination inside your head that you experience, but the reality that you have creatively visualized to capitulate your inner self to reach through the projection of thought power.

I recall the early writing of the white witch and psychologist Sybil Leek, who commented on how the first person to step foot on the moon should recognize that others had ventured there first—out of body. Travel is simply easier when you leave all of your physical baggage behind.

So, if we want to discover where we have been and where we are going in the long journey of our eternal soul, perhaps we should consider the words of Theosophist and psychic author Helena Blavatsky. Blavatsky reflected in *The Secret Doctrine* and a pamphlet on astrology that people whom we encounter on our world today probably lived earlier lives on Venus or Mars and likely will reincarnate to live again on distant planets. After all, our life force is not physically bound to one temporal location but can roam freely. It only follows that the life force within us, our inner spirit, can visit exotic locations where it has been or will one day live again. It needs only the opportunity and a little direction to make the journey now.

Certainly, it would be helpful to know about our earlier lives and our future lives as well, to help us understand the destiny of our human soul and to awaken to the inner drive that has propelled us on the arc of our journey. Our extended journey could prove more meaningful than the heroic adventure of Odysseus to find Ithaca.

Journey to Alternate Universes and Alternate Realities

While there is a limit to how far we can see and travel in our physical world, there is literally no limit to our reach into unseen parallel universes and realities. These lie beyond our physical vision and ability to measure in the material world we know. These are beyond our three-dimensional reality. Simply because they exist outside our physical eyesight, however, does not mean that they do not exist. Indeed, there is a full range of colors and musical notes beyond the limitations of our physical senses to perceive.

I always think of an inventor I interviewed once for a regional magazine. When I asked him how he could visualize things that did not exist and applications that nobody had considered before, he told me to lie on my back on the floor. Then he asked me to identify things on top of the coffee table near where I reclined. Because they were out of my sight, I could not see them or even speculate on what was there. He said that was the way most people go through life, seeing only things in clear sight at arm's length, while visionaries attempt to see beyond.

This assessment is similar to what P. D. Ouspensky described in *Tertium Origanum*. He explained how people in a second-floor apartment with no open windows or open doors were blinded to anything on the floors above or below them or anything outside the building beyond their shuttered windows. In a sense, then, we live in a box that we measure side to side, up and down, and in terms of depth as we perceive it. We then conclude that that is all there is to our world. This analysis is similar to Plato's Allegory of the Cave, where people were confused by what they saw from the dark recesses of their position within the cave.

But cutting-edge theoretical physicists, such as Nima Arkani-Hamed, Savas Dimopoulous, and Georgi Dvali, have explained that there is much more, which they described as "The Universe's Unseen Dimensions" in *Scientific American* (August 2000). Like other modern physicists, they argue that there are many parallel universes and realities, perhaps as close to us as the other side of a folded paper map. Indeed, the multiverse theory of parallel universes and realities is gaining ground in academic fields today. There is so much that we cannot see with our physical eyes or measure with our little tape measures.

In a consciousness energy body, however, we do not need to see around corners or folds in space, since physical barriers are no longer our barriers. Ouspensky's advice to a boxed-in, restricted view of the totality of what is around us was simply to attain an altered state of consciousness to project ourselves outside the box in which we live.

I am happy to report to you, as one person who has escaped the box in an altered state of consciousness, that there are an unlimited number of new things to see outside the physical planet on which your body resides. In self-programmed lucid dreams, I have risen far above the house in which my body safely rested, to distant heights in realms far beyond the ground that we commonly call the whole world. I have explored the seven heavens and examined what awaits us on the other side. I have crossed bridges to new realities where advanced spirits sing new worlds into creation and lovingly project new souls on waves of discovery into material incarnations.

And having done that, I believe that it is always good, in a sense, to see where our bread is baked and how it is packaged. Consequently, I am always eager to explore where we have originated and what awaits us in our endless journey of discovery. Our spirit longs to discover and yearns to grow. So why do we keep it hidden deep inside us?

Journey into the Past

Your travel in an out-of-body lucid dream can even take you into the past. In your energy body as pure consciousness, you are no longer restricted to your physical fixation in the here and now as your only recognizable point in the endless timeline. You can jump onto any portion of the timeline, as long as you visualize it on your clear blank slate that you prepare as a map for your journey. As the saying goes, if you can see it, then you can be it. You can be in the Middle Ages, in Atlantis, or in your past lives. The past is yours to explore.

In fact, it is shortsighted of us to think of it as some time that is past. The past, present, and future all are actively occurring on the common timeline. It is our sad limitation as physical beings that we can fix our perception on only one time and place.

There are many documented, researched cases of time travel by people who clearly reported visiting places in the past. In *Time Shifts*, an earlier book on time travel, I recounted famous cases of a group of scouts, two college professors, and two policemen that are pretty hard to refute for their collaboration and verifiability. One thing I noted is that these people, for the most part, became very quiet as they slipped in time, suggesting that they entered an altered state of consciousness.

The 1957 episode of a time-traveling group of scouts was described in depth by Mike Dash in *Smithsonian* magazine, researched in depth by Andrew MacKenzie of Psychical Research in the United Kingdom and later chronicled in the 1997 book *Adventures in Time*. The British lads were naval cadets taxed with finding the Suffolk village of Kersey in a field exercise to test their ability to read and follow a current map. All the boys claimed for years, however, that the Kersey they found was a plague-stricken village in the Middle Ages.

Another well-documented case of a time shift involved two academic women from Oxford University who visited the Palace of Versailles in 1901. There they found the Petite Trianon Garden occupied by people frozen in a scene from an earlier time. They reported that these people were wearing costumes and apparently celebrating some sort of garden party. They noted a woman sketching, later suggested to conform to descriptions of Marie Antoinette. It is known that she spent much time in this garden with friends centuries earlier. The two academic women continued to walk through the gardens, unnoticed and without engaging any of the characters there. They described a small bridge that was no longer present in 1901 but was later confirmed to have been present there centuries earlier.

There were very few people visiting the Palace of Versailles at the time that Charlotte Moberly, president of Oxford's St. Hugh's College, and colleague Eleanor Jourdain took their quiet garden stroll into the past. The professors revisited the gardens many times but never encountered what they had seen on that quiet day in 1901. They continued to tell their strange story and released a book titled *An Adventure* in 1911 to describe their adventure into the past. Later, the British Society for Psychical Research studied their account and was able to verify the strange bridge they saw, as well as the costume party organized by French poet Robert de Montesquiou as historically factual.

The *Liverpool Echo* reported the strange case of an alley thief who was chased by a policeman in 2006. The policeman reported that the thief vanished before his eyes. The thief later told the police that he stumbled into a scene from the past when he made his way to the end of the side street. There he saw many old shops that he did not recognize. He said he stopped at a newsstand, where he saw a newspaper with a dateline in 1967. The thief was startled by what he saw, he said, and turned to run back the way he had entered the scene out of time. There a surprised policeman grabbed him and took him in for questioning. Strangely, the description the thief gave police upon interrogation conformed to exactly the way the shops on that street once appeared during the 1960s.

There are actually many documented cases of time shifts, several of which are backed by government reports, studies, and collaboration. The point that should be made here is that time shifts seem to occur randomly. Quiet people on a stroll seem to enter an altered state, perhaps during electromagnetic fluctuations in the earth. These accounts sound dreamlike, similar to lucid dreaming. Unlike lucid dreaming, though, they are slips in time without programming as during conscious dreamwork.

Dreamwork, when programmed consciously, offers many exciting opportunities to explore alternate points on the eternal timeline. Most people would like to explore their past lives, or life between lives, to better understand the direction of their life's path now and throughout eternity. Many people might want to examine friends, relatives, and key characters who have helped shape their lives today. It would also be practical to observe key events in history in a state of heightened awareness, to study how it has impacted our present lives.

It is possible for you to visit any person, event, or place in history that you choose by visualizing it on the clear blank slate in front of your mind's eye as part of the dreamscape that you have planned. You can use that agenda as an unerring map to take you where and when you want to go. Spirit knows the way.

Journey into the Future

The same approach can be taken to visualize a picture of what time you want to visit in the future. You must recognize that many people do that in their lucid dreams, as proven by the many cases of precognitive dreams. Many people have dreams of the future that prove to be accurate. Evidently, they have witnessed the future. The future exists as another "now" on the endless time loop. We spend our physical lives focused on the ground in front of our feet in the here and now, so we never focus our intent on consciously visiting any other time.

In my book *Time Shifts*, I describe people who have traveled into the future during quiet moments. One well-documented case is that of Royal Air Force marshal Sir Victor Goddard in Scotland in 1935. His strange flight was researched by author Stephan Wagner. Goddart apparently saw the future of aviation when he flew over an abandoned airfield during a storm. When he passed over the same airfield on his return flight, however, he saw strange modern planes on a busy airfield and a ground crew wearing blue uniforms he had never seen before. Years later, the Scottish air force did indeed populate that airfield with the sort of yellow planes that Goddard had sighted years earlier, and switched uniforms of the ground crew from brown coveralls to the same blue outfits that Goddard had reported in his flight report.

The strange story of Rudolph Fentz, who died mysteriously in New York in 1950, is another well-documented case of time travel. A man with Victorian clothes and handlebar mustache suddenly appeared in busy New York traffic, apparently confused by cars. When he was killed in traffic, he became a mystery. On his body were very odd coins, a Philadelphia livery bill, and a card that simply read "Dr. Rudolph Fentz." Police received no report of missing persons after many days of searching for clues but did locate a Mrs. Rudolph Fentz in a local phone book. The woman reported that her deceased husband, Rudolph Fentz Jr., often spoke of his father's odd disappearance when he went for a quiet stroll one night decades earlier and never returned. He was apparently a dapper man in his Victorian suit with a handlebar mustache. He was a medical doctor known as Dr. Rudolph Fentz.

Obviously, people do sometimes glance into the future and even visit it in their dreams, as demonstrated by prophetic dreams. This demonstrates how departures into what we commonly called the future are not only possible but probable. We have proof that people have done it. Therefore, a lucid dream can be programmed objectively to include a journey into the future.

Personally speaking, I find it appealing to travel into the future to see how my life is progressing. If I see something that distresses me, I might be able to course-correct to avoid the direction I seem to be headed. In this way, I might be able to favorably change my future. I do not consider that morally wrong, since it involves only me. I should be able to set the course for my own life. Certainly, I have a karmic connection to myself in the past and in the future.

We must also recognize that the past is not written in stone, if we can course-correct on the basis of how energy appears to be shaping things in the future. Many ripples in time can affect what we commonly call our future. But what we see is the way that present energy seems to be shaping tomorrow.

It might seem even more difficult to accurately visualize the future on our blank slate and draw the future as a destination for us today. Indeed, it is difficult for temporal, mundane physical beings such as ourselves to grasp the concept that we can visit the future at all, since we tend to see it as being not yet in existence. But we must remember that the looped timeline is like a conveyor belt that we can step aboard at any point along its loop through space. We can simply draw something on our clear blank slate that our inner spirit will recognize as an abstract picture of the future we wish to visit. When spirit is ready to depart, it will follow the slate that we have created in our mind's eye as an unerring map.

CHAPTER 12

Confidence in Your Security and Safe Return

If we are truly honest with ourselves, we must admit that a lucid dream actually transports us outside the physical body in an altered state of heightened consciousness beyond ordinary time and space. It is not, therefore, simply imaginary thoughts inside our heads during sleep. That is an important concession that we must make and believe in order to fully appreciate and explore the dreamscape that we visit.

It also might seem frightening or challenging to some people who worry about leaving the body and traveling through time and space. I fully recognize, therefore, that some readers might want to hold back. This is a mistake and a hindrance to fully embracing the lessons of the dream.

The importance of the insights one can gain as gifts of the spirit in its outbound journey during lucid dreaming necessitates establishing complete comfort and security in the process. Otherwise, the gatekeeper function of the analytical mind will prevent you from ever leaving on this voyage of discovery.

This chapter, then, seeks to put any lingering concerns to the side and to establish a blanket of security and comfort for you to fully embrace your newfound freedom of discovery in lucid dreaming. We will offer added layers of assurance to allow you to leave your physical body and the present time and place of your material form far behind.

Secure a Safe Launching Pad

If the body and physical mind sense that they are secure and safe, then getting permission from the gatekeeper that holds you back should become easier. The analytical mind or brain within us will not allow any part of you to explore anywhere or anytime that it might consider potentially dangerous. It is concerned primarily with your physical safety.

Consequently, you can sideline its concerns by selecting a place to begin your lucid dream that is a safe point of departure, allowing the body to be protected and unthreatened during the temporary shutdown of the mind.

We cannot overestimate the importance of preparing a safe and protected location for you to put the body to rest, enter a state of heightened awareness, and leave in a conscious energy body, with the physical body limp on the ground behind you.

This should be a room that is pleasant and quiet, without any interruption. It should be private to ensure the body will not be disturbed. It should include a comfortable pad, mat, or bed on which you can recline to allow the body and mind to rest peacefully. If you opt to sit in a chair during your lucid dream, then securing a solid straight-back chair would be appropriate.

You might even lock the door or have a door guard, recognizing that a person who guards your door might best be positioned outside the room in which you recline. That way, you do not have any near and present perception of another person to distract you.

Prepare a Good Map

A clear map that you draw for your outbound journey will ensure that you are comfortable and secure in where you are going. This should not be rushed or hurried, since you have all the time in the world at your disposal. The completeness of your map as drawn on the clear blank slate before your mind's eye assures your consciousness that spirit has a specific time and place to land outside the physical body.

The directions that you draw need not be precise, but simply a sketch, like directions that you might draw on a napkin. So, you need not worry that it looks incomplete. The most important factor is that your spirit has a sense of direction. It is focused intent that draws this map, and your spirit can read it as an outline drawn by itself for itself to follow.

Tucking this map into the back of your consciousness while you prepare yourself with the posthypnotic command to recall it and follow it outside the body does essentially two things as helpful preparation. It allows you to prepare for departure and also assures your inner self that it is totally in control at this point in setting up the lucid dream. It is like shifting gears in your car into neutral to prepare and then shifting into drive to depart. It provides you a sense of being fully present and in command of the movement of your vehicle. In this case, the vehicle that is engaged and put into drive is your energized consciousness, which we recognize as spirit leaving the physical body, which ordinarily limits us to a parked position.

Assure Yourself on Arrival at the Dreamscape

Spirit can quickly leave the body with energized intelligence and arrive instantaneously at your designated time and place as mapped for your intended dreamscape. You must be prepared in advance for this sudden shift, so preparing yourself to depart with full permission and intent to follow the map you have drawn becomes your key to feeling comfortable upon arrival at your dreamscape, wherever you choose to go.

Even so, it can prove unsettling at first to suddenly find yourself out of time and space at an exotic dreamscape, even one you carefully selected and programmed with focused intent. Therefore, you need to fully acquaint yourself with your new surroundings and make yourself comfortable there, particularly in early lucid dreams. This is an important part of owning the scene and realizing meaningful insight, as you recognize that you truly belong there and find yourself on the right track.

Many guidebooks for dreaming suggest that you initially study the back of your hands to assure yourself that you are really in this dreamscape. This advice might help to assure you of your presence; however, I would add that in a typical lucid dream, you will not have physical hands to examine. You will have an etheric body, which is a double of your physical body. The etheric body is sort of an envelope between the physical body and astral or emotional body. It is a basic blueprint of your material body but might appear slightly larger and more ethereal when outside the realm of the physical body when it combines with the astral body, mental body, causal body, and more-spiritual bodies that surround you like a luminous egg.

It is quite possible that nobody in your dreamscape will take notice of you in your energy body, since you will lack material form that is familiar to people. In the material world, we basically view light reflected off solid objects as a way of seeing. You are more than a reflection of light here. You are energetically present.

You should spend some time orienting yourself to your new surroundings by owning your new set of eyes, new set of ears, new way of feeling, and other aspects of acute awareness that have now replaced your five physical senses. Scuba divers need to reorient themselves to new ways for breathing and moving the first time they descend to new ocean depths. This period of adjustment is equally important for a person in an early lucid dream.

In becoming comfortable in your new environment, you should next assess the characters, location, situation, and time you now occupy in your lucid dream. Yes, you have intentionally programmed this scene, but now you need to recognize that you are truly in this scene and honor its validity for your dream experience. If you think of this as a classroom situation that you have programmed for your special insight into matters that mean a lot to you, then this scene takes on special relevance to you as insightful. Therefore, you must make it yours.

There might be a temptation for you to attempt to interact upon arrival at your dreamscape, but for many people this will not prove possible. What seems to prevent that is the lack of recognition of the dreamer by others in this scene, in most cases. It is not your physical place in time, but a place that you now occupy in a vague energy body that most people will not recognize.

And even if you could interact, it would not be wise to do so. You are present at this point in the space-time continuum to observe and learn, bringing back insights from what you witness there. So, you are there as an objective observer with keen powers of awareness in your consciousness body.

An additional problem with attempting to interact would be a moral concern that you are disrupting the established timeline and events. This is not your physical point in time. This is a point that you are observing quietly, much as a shaman might do in visiting ancestors or going forward in time to see what awaits his people. If you watch carefully with new eyes and listen carefully with new ears, you can bring back helpful insights to guide you in your life path and overarching mission. And, yes, it is harder to listen when you are talking. So simply listen and learn.

Recognize That You Can Easily Leave and Return

It is essential for your sense of comfort to recognize that you can easily leave the dreamscape when you have observed what you intended to learn there. It will be equally easy for you to return in a future lucid dream that you program.

If you feel secure in the sense that you know you can easily return to your physical body and then revisit that exact time and place in a subsequent self-directed lucid dream, then you are in a good space to begin your insightful observation. It must be said that persons who are worried about getting home and worried about ever finding the same place again could be saddled with concerns that hold them back. Have you ever gone on a vacation to an exotic place far from the world you know so well, but you find yourself ridden with little worries about the trip? Do you worry whether you will be able to see everything that you came to explore and still able to catch the boat back? Will you be able to find your way around this exotic place without getting lost? Will you have trouble understanding things in this new place? You can hardly focus on the amazing experience that is now available to you when you worry about travel arrangements and how you can get around.

Rest assured that the inner self that has roamed far from your physical body instinctively knows how to get back without a hitch and can always return to this dreamscape. What makes this possible in part is your karmic connection to your two halves, like ends of the magnet that sense and are drawn to the complementary half. You always have an electromagnetic attraction to your subtle energy bodies and aspects of yourself that brings you together instantly. This is the totality of your whole self, your inner connectedness. Consider the study of natural connectedness described in such groundbreaking books by Peter Tompkins as *The Secret Life of Plants* and *Secrets of the Soil,* which demonstrate how parts of a whole sense the distant presence of other parts of the whole. These books led to new study of the connectedness of cells in the human body and the understanding that one cell in the physical body senses and identifies with other cells within the body.

I would suggest that this connectedness in identity is a constant throughout creation, with awareness on all levels of being. It is not just a physiological reality or a reality in the material world. In the case of bilocation of a person in a lucid dream, one-half of you will sense the other half even across distances to rejoin instinctively like ends of a magnet.

This is the same karmic connection and karmic attraction that allows us to easily find our self in past and future lives, since these also demonstrate aspects of the totality of your whole being.

Internalize the Message upon Your Return

There is a definite warm glow that radiates across your entire body from the inside out when you have fully integrated the message that you sought in a programmed dream. It will bring comfort to you and a sense of security that the dreamscape that you visit in your lucid dream is actually a safe and friendly place with benefits for you.

This is good on two levels, actually. There is that tingling glow of satisfaction that comes from having attained a new level of insight. That tingling, warm sensation that runs throughout your total being is the same sensation you might have experienced earlier during insight. You might recall the hair on the back of your neck tingling with joy upon learning something profound that made you feel more complete. Most likely, it was a magical moment for you. Your probing intuition has paid off and given you insights that you could only dream about encountering.

The second level of satisfaction from internalizing an insightful message in a dream comes from your physical side. That comes upon return from the dreamscape after the message of what you learned has been fully integrated into your total being. At this juncture, your analytical mind comes to appreciate the value of letting your inner consciousness roam. Your physical mind can now understand without further reservation that your out-of-body travel during physical rest can be worthwhile on a grand scale. A total body awareness of the value of a lucid dream for what the journey out of body brings back is like discovering newfound treasure. Like the arc of a hero's journey, the planned out-of-body adventure of a dreamer places a person in supernatural scenarios in another world that challenge the person to learn. The treasures of such a voyage of discovery are not gold, but invaluable knowledge that is won. It is transformational knowledge, as powerful as the alchemist's claims of turning base matter into gold.

We cannot underestimate the value of this insight. It is truly what the journey is all about. You might want to try setting up a programmed lucid dream simply for the adventure and joy that such an exotic out-of-body experience offers. But the thrill is a passing sense of appreciation. What lasts much longer and has far-greater value is the insight of what you can learn by carefully planning a lucid dream. The discovery is always more important than the destination. And the greatest find involves personal enrichment in the dreamer's self-discovery along the way.

The treasures found in the dreamscape, then, are priceless pieces to bolster the soul. They will make you more than you were, and bring you closer to self-realization and spiritual evolution in your grand mission that never ends.

To put these pieces of insightful information into you to bolster you on the deepest level of your soul, however, you must internalize the message of what you have learned in your lucid dream. If you cannot identify the treasure and put it to good use on a personal level, it is not transformational. Therefore, the information gathered in your lucid dream should be processed and integrated upon return from the dreamscape. This means that dreamers must be able to make newfound information an essential part of their total being. The information should resonate harmonically throughout their whole being on all levels. This makes you more complete and whole.

Due to the high stakes of finding, securing, and processing the information that is available in a lucid dream, the dreamer should carefully meditate what has been learned upon return to the physical body. The insights cannot be forgotten or lost. They cannot be confused by mental analysis but must first be assimilated into the core of your inner self and added to your heightened consciousness.

As you internalize the message in this way, you become the sum of what you have learned, with new insight that helps you evolve. The insights of what you have processed in your lucid dream then become an integral part of you and your true self, your inner self. You own the information and become one with the information.

CHAPTER 13

The Never-Ending Journey of the Hero within You

If we properly treat the lucid dream as an out-of-body journey of spirit into a new world of discovery, this makes our dreamscape much like the arc of a hero's journey in classical literature and psychology. Consequently, we should analyze what the classical hero's journey looks like and what it offers. That will give us some scope as to how important the lucid dream can be to us and our development.

The classical arc of a hero's journey is a thing of legend and grand proportions for what it delivers to the serious traveler. It is more than adventure. It is a call to action, filled with numerous supernatural encounters that offer insight, self-discovery at every turn, and opportunity for transformation. One finds treasures along the way, gifts of the spirit, and a promise of completion and spiritual wholeness.

Consider Dorothy in the land of Oz. She is carried on a challenging journey of great discovery in an exotic land. Mostly what she discovers in meeting the challenge in this strange land are insights into her. She must pass a gatekeeper to advance and then battle supernatural foes and conditions that challenge her to grow and learn. Along the way, she finds benefits not only for herself but also her loved ones, as she develops a heroic sense of community service. She returns home and finds that she has changed upon her return, due to the completion of the arc of her journey, which made her whole.

Homer's classic Greek tale of Odysseus is similar, demonstrating that an athletic king needs the challenge to grow as much as a little girl off the farm. Odysseus accepts the call to embark from the known world to an unknown world, challenged by supernatural forces at every turn. He grows from overcoming these obstacles and becomes transformed. He ultimately receives treasures more valuable than any chest of gold and receives blessings from a goddess as favorable winds to complete the final leg of his circumnavigation of the high seas. His return home to Ithaca is almost anticlimactic, since he has become whole and ripe with wisdom from the long journey. This is more than an exciting sea story. It is a journey of self-discovery and a search for wholeness.

The heroic prince in *The Bhagavad Gita* enters a long war with a supernatural guide to show him the real challenges and insights of growing personally in difficult circumstances. He becomes a more whole person with self-discovery won during many battles. These confrontations on the fields far from the safety of his home produce more than battle victories of war. They allow him to study things in greater depth, so that he emerges from war a better man.

To make our journeys of spirit in lucid dreaming epic in proportion and part of our transformation, we should analyze what makes the arc of a hero's journey and why it is important here. Once we consider the elements of the hero's journey, we will recognize that every lucid dream we plan and execute with focused intent is a personal journey of the inner hero inside us.

Leaving the Known World Behind

The classical hero in the arc of a hero's journey always leaves the known world behind to embark on an uncertain adventure into the unknown. This is precisely what the lucid dreamer does in leaving the comfortable surroundings of the physical world behind to journey out of body behind familiar time and space. Often this is done with childlike enthusiasm and a lack of fear, like a fool on a journey. The traveler is hoping to discover something in this exotic travel into the unknown and jumps off familiar surroundings with a desire to find a better world on a personal level and for the greater good. We laugh at Don Quixote but still consider the Fool in the Tarot deck a beneficial card to draw for people who are trying to find their way.

Granted, a lucid dream can be carefully planned, so that the dreamer has some knowledge of what lies ahead in the way a map is drawn. Still, the dreamer is a bit like Don Quixote jumping off the known world into less familiar realms. The known world of the dreamer is hard ground felt by two feet, while the unknown world is the less traveled realms of spirit outside normal space and time.

Accepting the Call to Action

The classical hero in the arc of a hero's journey must willingly accept the call to advance before fully engaging on the path. Many people hear the call to action but shy away. This is a bold journey that you must take on your own. It is easier to reject the call and stay home in the known world with its comfortable familiarity. It is a stretch to accept the challenge and begin the hero's journey of discovery.

Similarly, many people are challenged to accept a call to assume daring lives in the physical world, assuming personal challenges on unfamiliar terrain that could benefit others and offer individual growth. These life paths seem too dangerous for many, so they do not heed the call and remain in the known world off the challenging path.

The lucid dreamer who self-directs a planned dreamscape outside known space and time must be similarly focused. The purposeful dreamer must deeply want, with intent and deep desire, such an adventure outside the known world. The dreamer must be willing to jump off the world, much like Dorothy was carried far from Kansas and then given the choice to follow a strange and winding yellow brick road into the unknown.

While some people might suddenly find themselves in a lucid dream they did not plan, most people who purposefully do dreamwork will willingly accept the challenge to leave the known world with acute awareness.

Overcoming the Gatekeeper's Challenge

Soon after accepting the call and beginning the arc of the journey, the classical hero must overcome a gatekeeper. It is no different, perhaps, for the lucid dreamer on a journey beyond the known world. As we have suggested earlier, dreamers who desire to activate heightened consciousness to lead them into the unknown world outside the physical realm must first overcome the physical mind as gatekeeper. Dorothy, upon attempting to enter the Emerald City, had to convince the gatekeeper that her business in seeking entrance was "a horse of a different color." For the lucid dreamer who requires a pass beyond the gatekeeper, the task is to convince the possessive analytical mind to lower its guard to let conscious awareness pass into the unknown world. That, too, is a horse of a different color, since our mental controls do not ordinarily let such things pass. This is not overcoming the gatekeeper by force, but by reason. The mind must harmonically agree that the request is not an everyday request but is worth honoring. Recognizing a nonphysical, invisible intelligence deep inside its body, the mind has indeed seen a horse of a different color and realizes that it poses no threat in its request to advance beyond the gate it controls.

Supernatural Challenges

Once past the gatekeeper, the classical hero on the arc of a journey is bombarded at every turn along the winding path by supernatural challenges. Dorothy had to overcome powerful witches and flying monkeys, while Odysseus was confronted by powerful goddesses and gods of the sea, land, and air who tried to prevent his boat and crew from reaching their destination. Odysseus even traveled beyond death to visit the departed.

In considering supernatural challenges, however, we should think beyond personification of powerful forces as goddesses who stop the wind and gods who send storms. Rather, we should think of them as primordial powers present in nature. We cannot stop a storm or bend the wind to our will any more than we can overcome a god or goddess, as a rule. But the hero on the arc of a journey must do that to advance and gain personal power and insight.

The self-directed lucid dreamer confronts supernatural challenges in the journey outside the known world as well. Such dreamers escape from the physical confines of their dense material form and soar beyond normal time and space, bilocating with one foot in the present physical realm and one foot far above the clouds in exotic realms. To our common way of seeing things in our restrictive world of matter, that sort of adventure is supernatural and overcomes huge obstacles.

Mentors and Helpers

The classical hero on the arc of a journey will meet mentors and helpers along the way. The same is true of self-directed lucid dreamers who venture into the unknown world outside known time and space. Such mentors and helpers for the classical hero on a perilous journey of discovery might sometimes be hard to identify as allies, since help can come from the most-unlikely sources. The challenge is to spot the help and realize it when presented to you in any form, even disguised as a nagging old man or annoyance that is seemingly in your way.

The dream mentors and guides that one might likely encounter in a planned lucid dream will generally be easier to spot, particularly if the dreamer has visualized and manifested them as allies. It is also likely that a guide or teacher could pop into a lucid dream without advance notice, simply because spirit sees the need and urgently desires it.

Once arrived at the dreamscape, the dreamer might encounter unlikely help in the characters that are gathered there. In the case of a self-programmed lucid dream, the primary characters might already be determined by visualization and dream mapping. Nonetheless, there could be some notable surprises in who shows up at your dreamscape to enlighten you.

In the case of an unplanned lucid dream, the characters one encounters in a vivid scene are more unpredictable. You are almost certain to have helpers appear out of nowhere. Spirit calls them forth with a strong sense of desire and will to know. Consequently, everyone whom you are likely to encounter in a lucid dream should be carefully studied with acute awareness. Everyone you meet is likely to have important information to guide you.

Emerging a Transformed Person

At a pivotal point in the arc of a hero's journey, the hero descends to the point of no return and must encounter an abyss. There, the hero goes through a dark hour of the soul, emerging as a new person. Some would-be heroes, of course, cannot bear to face this depth and abandon the journey to return to the known world. While difficult, the abyss challenges the hero to undergo a massive transformation. It is like dying, in a sense, and being reborn. The rest of the journey will be as a new person with greater insight and awareness.

Similarly, lucid dreamers often find themselves out of their depth once they begin to dream-travel and go through something like a deep abyss. Once they have arrived at a dreamscape, they can work their way through it and master the situation as an acute observer with keen awareness.

Will they panic and find themselves troubled by being out of their normal depth? In the case of a self-directed lucid dream, dreamers have an advantage here. They know what is coming next and will not be as startled and threatened by what they find along the way. Even more than the accidental lucid dreamer who does not plan the dreamscape, they can emerge a transformed person in the journey. They know from the outset that they are entering a lucid dream to gain insight and seek transformation, so there are fewer surprises.

Treasures of the Journey

We always read in classical stories of the arc of a hero's journey about the amazing treasures discovered along the way. Heroes who complete the full arc of the journey will return with exotic treasures that are not found in their known world. Generally, these treasures are intrinsic and most valuable on a spiritual level as gifts of the spirit toward inner growth and enrichment.

Often, these special gifts are foretold to us in our buildup for the journey in the lucid dream. When we plan our own lucid dream, we draw a picture of what we want to see, where we want to go, and what we want to learn. This picture can include everything, including whom we want to observe, the situation we want to witness, and what we want to learn in our dreamscape. Consequently, a self-directed lucid dream will include a sort of wish list of what we desire to learn and achieve in our dream experience. The lucid dream, after all, is a learning dream. We visit dreamscapes outside normal space and time in dream scenarios that we program for an information-gathering experience. The drawing we prepare with our focused intention becomes our map. What we gather and what we learn in the dreamscape, therefore, become our special treasures.

A random lucid dream that we have not intentionally programmed might pose difficulties to gathering information and collecting treasures, since we have entered a dreamscape without a treasure map. Our inner spirit has hijacked us on a great adventure of personal discovery. Our inner self has jumped past the gatekeeper and taken us on the arc of our journey with an agenda of its own making. It knows what you want and what you need on the deepest level, having lived before this lifetime and knowing the future as your connection to greater consciousness. Spirit sets up your challenges and leads you to mentors and learning situations in this breakout vivid dream.

But once in the dreamscape of even a breakout dream that you have not intentionally planned, spirit has brought you there with acute awareness to see with new eyes and hear with new ears. Consequently, you can learn and retrieve special gifts of the soul in these dreamscapes as well. What insights you gather might not have been on some agenda that you drew in advance as your map, but you will be perfectly positioned once at your dreamscape to identify and retrieve special gifts that have proved unobtainable to you in the physical life.

Do you recall the Humphrey Bogart classic movie *The Treasure of the Sierra Madre*? The arc of this journey did not bring any actual gold to the hero but instead taught him about human nature. Always remember that the lucid dream, like the arc of a hero's journey, offers us self-discovery with special insights as its greatest treasure.

Gifts of the Goddess

Toward the end of the arc of a hero's journey, the transformed, insightful traveler might be rewarded in the home stretch with parting gifts from the goddess, thinking of *The Odyssey* and similar classics. This celebrates the hero's return from a successful journey. It honors the integrity, grit, and determination of the hero to complete the arduous trip in style. Literary scholars and psychologists have referred to this phase, dating back to early epics from Homer, as gifts of the goddess, although travelers might receive such supernatural gifts from other than a female deity, of course. Think of the successful batter who has hit a home run and is slapped on the back while running the final steps to home plate.

In the first phase of the arc of a hero's journey, the traveler is challenged by supernatural entities or forces but then receives supernatural assistance and congratulations on the home stretch after a journey well run.

The point, perhaps, is that the path becomes easier after successful completion of challenging tasks, and the universe rewards the hero who has run a good race. We might think of it as karmic reward to reinforce the wisdom of the choices made. It does not need to have the personification or face of a deity. It might fall gently upon our return like a feather from an unknown messenger flying far above us.

Certainly, things will go easier for us as we gain insight and secure greater inner strength and wisdom from what we learn in a lucid dream. We will sense that we are on the right path of self-discovery by how easy things might become as we perform our dreamwork.

Return Home

In the arc of the hero's journey, the traveler completes the full arc by returning home as a changed person. Much has been learned in the journey, and the hero is not the same person who left of the journey. Odysseus is not the same man when he finally returns home to Ithaca, and few outside his faithful dog even recognize him. Dorothy is told upon her return home that she just bumped her head and had a profound dream that wasn't real at all, although she returns with more information about her companions back in Kansas as a result of her "dream."

In the lucid dream, the traveler returns home in the sense that the consciousness returns to the physical body after visiting the dreamscape outside common space and time. But there is much more for us to consider here. Think of a baseball game in which every player has a chance at bat, followed by a chance to support others at bat, and then a chance to observe others from the field as they bat. Each player gets three strikes and a scenario that includes a full inning with three chances at bat for the team. If a player is successful at bat, then he or she rounds all the bases and returns home to try again. Even after three strikes and the side striking out three times, each player is afforded nine full innings for recurring attempts to succeed.

So it is with us. We will have many chances to journey beyond the known and challenge ourselves in difficult situations, even situations we program in intentional dreams. We might have many little victories, where we complete the journey immediately before us and have the wondrous experience of transformation to achieve a greater wholeness as a result. But the game is not over that soon. When we return home, we collect ourselves only long enough to prepare for our next insightful journey. Home, then, is a state of mind. It is home base. It is a pivotal point from which to embark.

Lucid dreaming can be repeated over and over, as we continually journey outside space and time to learn, challenge ourselves, and seek personal transformation through insight gained along the path. The journey never really ends, since we continue to grow and evolve. And spiritual evolution is endless.

CHAPTER 14

Dream Analysis and Journaling

We have touched on dream analysis and journaling previously, but now we will outline a more exacting procedure that should prove valuable to you on a daily basis in your serious dreamwork. I recognize that many people like to turn to popular dream dictionaries, psychologists, and other therapists to interpret the meaning of their dreams. Many will try to analyze the dream as best they can remember, by writing it all down in a dream journal and adding to that journal with each subsequent dream.

I confess that I worked previously for book publishers who produced dream dictionaries for people to look up imagery from what they remember in a dream to learn what it all means. I do not feel pride today in having helped produce these dream dictionaries.

What worries me about consulting dream dictionaries is that our dreams are highly subjective by nature and cannot be objectively evaluated by somebody who is far detached from you and knows nothing about you or your very personal dream. Producing a correspondence chart that identifies what various things in a dream means suggests that everyone is having the same dream and has the same life. Each one of us, of course, is unique. Adding to the confusion is the fact that many of the popular dream dictionaries in circulation today contradict each other.

So who is right? Who knows what your dreams really mean? I would suggest that it is not some writer who banged off an index of images that might or might not appear in anyone's dreams.

The best person to interpret your very personal dreams is always you. Understanding the dream is an important part of your dreamwork. People for many centuries and in various cultures have practiced serious dreamwork as a doorway for the inner self to explore and learn. I have outlined some of this history in *Ancient Wisdom Scrolls, Lucid Dreams* (REDFeather, 2022).

While ancients even erected dream temples with assistants to facilitate the dreaming experience, the practice of dreaming has always been personal. There are legends of ancient dream oracles that confused people by their vague pronouncements. Nobody knows you better than your inner self knows you. This is the part of you that leaves the physical body with energized consciousness.

Now, we must be careful here to distinguish again between common dreams of the restless mind and lucid dreams of discovery. In terms of dream review and journaling, the two types of dreams should be treated differently.

Dream Dictionaries for the Common Restless Dream

Admittedly, it makes a little more sense to consult outside help to analyze a common dream that a person experiences randomly during restless sleep, when the physical mind continues to mull over past problems and future worries that have not been resolved in more-waking hours. Sometimes, these are nightmares. Many people commonly endure these fitful memories drudged up by the restless mind.

Because people find such restless dreams troublesome, they seek to pinpoint what they mean. It is basic human nature to want to measure things, so that we feel that we have gained some measure of control over conditions that impact us. So they try to look up what images in their restless dream really meant.

Now, there is probably a lot of similarity to the way our physical minds work, but we must also recognize that each of us has a unique history and circumstances that make a generalized identification of our inner thoughts difficult. And have you noticed how jumbled and confused your random restless dreams are? Your half-asleep brain is plugging away at half speed in attempts to resolve problems that confounded it even when fully alert.

Nonetheless, dream dictionaries are generally written with these common restless dreams in mind, as a possible crutch for people who are vexed by troublesome images when they are trying to sleep peacefully at night. They are not primarily written as a guide for lucid dreamers, who are using dreams to address inner needs through intentional, focused dreamwork.

Psychological Analysis of Restless Dreams

Professional analysis by psychologists, psychotherapists, and others honestly seeks to unravel the mystery of muddled dreams that trouble people on restless nights when the mind cannot let go of concerns of the day. Since these restless dreams upset people, causing psychological damage, they probably need to be addressed in some way. The approach in psychology is that the restless mind is a window to what bothers you, screaming for attention. When individuals have recurring dreams that upset them and wake them with a start, then it becomes a concern of physical health as well. Troublesome dreams such as that can interfere with peaceful sleep cycles and put bags under your eyes.

As a result, there is an obvious call for professional counseling to deal with recurring restless dreams that trouble individuals. How help may be achieved for the troubled person depends on many variables, many of which are outside the control of the therapist. To gain some control over the dream, therapists might put the patient in a comfortable position that resembles a sleeping position. They will coach the patient to try to recall the dream and describe it. They might induce a sort of meditation trance or even use hypnosis in attempts to get the patient to return to the dream and describe it in detail.

Such clinical therapists often are concerned with what has happened at an earlier time in life, perhaps in childhood, when something seemed to confuse or bother the person. As a result, they want to unlock the mysteries of troublesome dreams of past scenarios that prevent someone from seeking peace and rest during sleep. They will try to regress the person to relive dreams or a point in a lifetime when keys to dream worries might be found.

But we are focused in this book on lucid dreams of discovery, not confusion. Also, we are focused on dreams that take us much further back than our childhood or into our future.

Writing Down Your Restless Dreams

Dream journals can become a good register to record your restless dreams to review a pattern and try to understand them. Many people keep a bedside spiral notebook or blank paper with a pen or pencil, ready to record everyday dreams. After a while, these regular dreams will display a sort of pattern that can be analyzed. In that manner, everyday dreamers can hope to determine what concerns keep them tossing and turning night after night.

The dream journal, then, can be used to see what sort of problems call out for attention, even if they are difficult to interpret. Clearly, if people knew the answers to problems that bother them, even in restless dreams, they could grasp the problem and dissect it to end their endless grief. But the best they can hope to do, perhaps, is to determine a pattern to their common, restless dreams and try to identify what the underlying problem is. Unfortunately, the analytical mind already senses the problem but cannot solve it. Otherwise, it would put the issue to rest and stop rehashing it during sleep.

This sort of practical dream journal becomes a diary of the dreams we cannot stop, the dreams that keep coming back when we are trying to forget the worries of the day but cannot let go of deeper concerns. Therefore, it is a deeply personal diary of your innermost thoughts that you might hope to identify and possibly resolve.

Before dream journaling, the dreamer might want to remain quiet and still in the sleeping position to try to hold the images of the dream in memory. It might help to try to lightly meditate on the dream, although it becomes evident to many that a random, common dream of a restless night is really more the domain of a foggy physical brain than our inner consciousness. After all, this was a muddled stumbling inside your head, not an outbound journey of discovery of the spirit. So it is ultimately left for the muddled mind to try to unravel its own muddled thinking during a hazy evening.

Self-Analysis of Your Lucid Dreams

The situation is vastly different with a lucid dream, which is driven by your inner consciousness and not by your restless mind. The agenda and goals are particularly clear in a lucid dream that you have programmed in advance with focused intent.

Upon return from a lucid dream—often in an exotic place and time outside your physical memory, the dreamer can remain quiet and still for a period of reflection and meditation on the dream scenario. Meditation in this instance should prove fruitful, since the lucid dream intimately involved the heightened consciousness of your inner spirit. Hence, spirit can identify the elements of the dreamscape as an active participant. Spirit also possesses the acute awareness of observation that it brings to the dream and returns from the dream with awareness.

It is heightened consciousness that allows us to meditate, so this approach for self-processing of the lucid dream has an excellent chance of success. We must always remember that spirit knows everything about you, far beyond the limited scope of your analytical brain, which relies on memories that are often flawed. Mental memories are often muddled by the lack of acute awareness of our sensory perception and our physical ability to understand things outside our physical scope of experience.

When the lucid dreamer has quietly taken the opportunity upon return to the physical body to review and hold the dream, then the dreamer can accurately occupy the dream with the acute awareness of heightened consciousness in meditation.

Recoding Lucid Dreams in a Dream Diary

After meditating on the lucid dream, the dreamer can reliably record an outline of the dreamscape in a dream diary. Upon making a diary entry, the active mind might be tempted to attempt to analyze the lucid dream on paper.

This could be difficult and perhaps even a mistake. It is like asking someone who speaks only French to try to analyze a conversation overheard in Spain. It might seem vaguely familiar but will not easily translate. Your physical mind is clearly out of its element to analyze a lucid dream to which it was not really present.

It should be enough that heightened consciousness has processed the lucid dream and tucked it away deep in your inner self, a place where the physical mind has little familiarity. Maybe the best that can be done in recording a lucid dream in a dream dictionary would be to outline the dreamscape by identifying the time, place, and events that unfolded in the dreamscape, without analysis.

In this manner, the dream dictionary holds an outline of the dreamscape, complete with characters and situations in the lucid dream. Lucid dreams that are continuations of earlier dreams can be added to the appropriate entry and cataloged in the journal to determine a pattern. Therefore, your dream journal can show progress in developing a theme, leaving analysis to the heightened spirit that dwells within us.

CHAPTER 15

Shared Dreams

There are a number of viable ways for you to share a lucid dream, and good reasons to consider it on occasion. First, we should clarify what a shared dream really is and what it is not. We are not here considering how you might subsequently discuss a lucid dream that you have experienced with another person after the dream. We do not mean sharing the dream in that sense. No, we are focusing our attention here on lucid dreams that you jointly experience with another dreamer who joins you in the common dreamscape. In a real sense, then, you are dreaming together and experiencing essentially the same dream at the same time.

You could program the same agenda and mapping with someone you want to join you in your dream. The two of you could agree to find each other in the same lucid dream. You could even meet with several like-minded people in a common dreamscape. Admittedly, the arc of the journey of discovery in dreamwork is basically a solo adventure, but there are times when you might want to join others, for reasons we will examine. Of course, this is a personal choice and one that would involve others who must also elect to join you.

We say that dreamwork is basically a solo adventure of self-discovery for good reason. This is a track of challenge and individual learning that your inner spirit is compelled to experience in order to grow and become whole. While everyone has the opportunity to accept the challenge of this dreamwork and walk this similar path, no two people walk it exactly the same way. Everyone's learning curve is different. We have individual needs. We all learn at a different pace and in different ways. Some people learn better by hearing, while others learn best by seeing or experiencing. This is not the same as suggesting that some people are more advanced or even better students. It just suggests that we are slightly different and unique as individuals. Yet, we all walk a similar path. We just walk it at a different pace with different observations along the way, as the path beckons to each of us according to our desires and needs as individuals. Consequently, the course might appear slightly different, depending on who is walking the course and what that individual is compelled to experience at this point of development.

Shared Thought Forms

We can on occasion, however, share a dream experience with another dreamer by merging our thought forms. It is our inner thoughts as projected consciousness that bring us to a specific dreamscape every time. Our conscious thoughts have a form of their own as intelligent energy and can be directed to a specific location. That is how we always reach our mark in following the map that we have drawn in advance to visualize precisely where and when we desire to go in our lucid dreams and what event or situation we desire to observe there.

In my earlier book *Manifesting* (REDFeather, 2021), I outlined how our conscious thoughts could be visualized and specifically targeted to bring us to a specific place, time, and situation—even though we are less than fully certain of the specifics. Spirit will find the way. It needs only intelligent energy to propel it to its mark.

This explains how we can link ourselves with people, places, times, and situations that are seemingly outside us and remote. Our consciousness as intelligent energy is really electromagnetic energy, the same universal force of primal source that propels and sustains all of life. It is present in all living things as a driving force and eternal being. The electromagnetic nature of this intelligent energy allows it to instinctively connect complementary components like two ends of a magnet. In this sense, we are never alone and isolated, but always connected to things that we identify strongly with. Our ability to visualize and project our thought power to find things and bring them to us is our magnetic ability as energy beings that are packaged in a protective physical body.

There is power in linking our thought power with others to give it greater impact and stronger fidelity. Consider for a moment the power in group prayer, meditation, singing, chanting, and study. It has a different feel, does it not? You can sense the others joining their thoughts as intelligent energy to your thought power. You can feel the group dynamics. This is true even when two people join their thoughts, particularly if the two people identify strongly with each other and sense a magnetic connection.

You can practice connecting your thought forms with another person before attempting to share a lucid dream. A practice session should prove helpful in gaining confidence that you can link with another person effectively. The setup to this exercise is similar to programming any lucid dream.

You can share the same room or recline in adjoining rooms. You could even coordinate the time you do this while in entirely different places. The important thing is that you start at the same time and with the same focus.

You either sit quietly in a straight-back chair, with erect posture and bare feet firmly grounded, or recline on your back, with arms and legs outstretched at 45-degree angles (preferred). You should wear loose-fitting, comfortable clothing, without any sort of jewelry, and not cross any part of your body, so that the intelligent energy can flow freely throughout you.

Then you want to put your physical body to rest by focusing on your feet up to your head, with the command to become heavy and go to sleep. Begin deep, rhythmic breathing and continue until it becomes automatic. Then tune out all exterior and interior thoughts until your physical mind is at rest. You should begin to sense a quiet stillness deep inside you. You should begin to feel your heightened consciousness racing faster and faster.

Visualize a clear blank slate in front of your mind's eye. Begin to draw a picture on this slate of your friend who is sharing this exercise with you. When the picture seems formed—even though sketchy—tuck it into the back of your consciousness to retrieve later as an instant road map. When it returns before your mind's eye, you will instantaneously use this drawing as an unerring map to take you to that person. Now in the void before your mind's eye, prepare yourself to leave your physical body as soon as the map is recalled. Give yourself permission to leave and go to that person. Then recall the drawing and feel yourself projected outward. You should begin to see your friend shortly.

You should agree on where both of you will be located when you go on your shared dream. Your spirits will find each other regardless. The most important thing is that both of you do this exercise together at the same time.

Afterward, the two of you can compare reports of what you experienced, to determine how successful you were in merging your thought forms. Were you able to see each other? Were you able to share thoughts? You can try this several times to perfect the process.

Of course, you could simply select something that would occupy your focus at the same time, without your full energy bodies visiting during dream setup. In this case, your consciousness could leave your body without your ethereal body and other subtle energy bodies. If you focus on a specific place to focus your attention, then you can visualize that place and what to think about. In such a case, you could link your thoughts with another person, as many people commonly do, without actually visualizing the person and visiting that person. Only your thoughts would reach the target, so you would need to discuss with your friend how successful each of you seemed to be in reaching your target and focusing your conscious thoughts on the subject.

I prefer to visualize my dream partner and draw a picture of that person to merge with my lucid dream. If you try this exercise, you should also agree with your friend where you might want to meet and what might consume your focused attention when you arrive at the targeted designation together. That complete approach will prepare you for all levels of future shared dreams.

You could do this exercise in a lucid dream that you program or do it in a waking meditation. The setup is basically the same.

Agreement to Meet at a Specific Time and Place

When you become comfortable with the concept of sharing a lucid dream with another person, you can become very specific in jointly agreeing on the time, place, and dreamscape scenario. You can even coordinate the characters you might want to include in your dreamscape, the scene, the event, and even the outcome that you seek. Always keep in mind that the situation you visualize and map for your programmed dream is a learning situation that you preestablish to offer you particular insight. Once you're at the dreamscape, it becomes your challenge to seize the opportunity to realize the significance of what you have carefully observed with the acute awareness of your focused consciousness.

It is conceivable that two people could agree to share a lucid dream with different agendas, since no two people have exactly the same background and needs. Nonetheless, the time, place, and situation that you have in mind for your learning experience would be the same. In fact, coming to a shared dreamscape with slightly different agendas offers you the opportunity to share what both of you have learned from the experience, thereby doubling your bounty of discovered insight.

It is highly likely, after all, that the two of you do not have exactly the same intention, since you do not have exactly the same needs. Therefore, spirit will naturally select points of insight from the dreamscape for each of you, even if you program the dreamscape identically. Back to our horse of a different color: think of yourself riding a pinto-colored quarter horse that stands 15 hands high, while your dreaming companion is riding a chestnut-colored thoroughbred that is 19 hands high. That comparison might suggest to you how different your spirits are, even though you want to arrive at the same time, place, and scene. Riding to your common designation on different horses, you will naturally see things differently from where you sit in the saddle.

Programming the Same Self-Directed Dream

If you tried the earlier exercise to share your conscious thought forms with another person through focused visualization, then you already have the basic outline of how to share a self-directed lucid dream with a friend. All that you need now is to program the same lucid dream in greater detail.

A lucid dream is based on a visualization and projected thought form, but it also has other programmed elements drawn by the dreamer to complete the mapping process. These detailed elements can be discussed in detail with your designated dream companion. In that manner, both of you can arrive at exactly the same dreamscape at the same time, with the same cast of characters, the same scene setup, and a similar lesson to be learned.

There is no telling, given the difference in the background and needs of the two dreamers, whether both parties at the dreamscape will make the same observations and leave the lucid dream with exactly the same insight. But they can always compare notes. And if they do intentionally focus on the same lesson plan with the same desired result, it is possible that they will have remarkably similar insights after the dream.

Consequently, there is potential power in shared dreaming, just as there is power in shared thought forms. If you share a similarly programmed lucid dream with another person, you could gain the power of two. The common experience gives both of you the chance to share observations. This could ultimately help both of you analyze the significance of what you have learned. Such analysis in jointly meditating on the dreamscape experience could prove invaluable.

Joining Your Twin Flame

A shared lucid dream with your twin flame could be intensely illuminating, since the doubling is even more personal and the shared insights even more impactful. Your twin flame could be your spiritual counterpart, a person who is closely associated with you through various lifetimes. Lucky is the person who has consciously met his or her twin flame, since often we encounter our opposite number during our lifetime without really identifying them as a significant aspect of our own life. Such a person could have been your spouse, child, or parent in a previous life. This person could have worked closely with you. This person is always aligned to you, although you might fail to recognize your twin flame even when near to you.

Please recognize that your twin flame is not necessarily your soulmate, but more like a working partner who sees you through many lifetimes. This is more like a yin-yang connection, a mirror image, a male-female connection, or poles of a magnet always drawn together through shared karma. Think of yourself as helpmates. You are going through life endlessly together at essentially the same pace, time, and place. Each of you is a flame of light that resembles the flame of light of the other. You are truly twins, and you naturally complement each other in profound ways eternally.

So when you share a lucid dream with your twin flame, it will be most profound and intense. Your joint presence will double the intensity that both of you receive from the insight. It will be more special that sharing a dream with anyone else.

Of course, it is obvious that most people do not necessarily know their twin flame in this lifetime to the degree they could contact them to coordinate a shared lucid dream. In such cases, you could visualize your twin flame abstractly and incorporate you conceptualized twin flame in one of your planned dreams. Without knowing your twin flame in the physical world, you would not be able to coordinate the dream with your twin. You would, however, be able to call them into your dream by visualizing your need to contact them in the blank slate before your mind's eye in creative visualization. Once you have called your twin flame into one of your lucid dreams, both of you might recognize each other from the dreamscape and actually locate each other physically outside the dream.

I have personally shared lucid dreams both with a close friend and also my twin flame. While you might program the dreamscape in careful cooperation to arrive at the same place with the same purpose in both cases, the experience with a twin flame could prove more intense and productive. You will share more of a common focus and intent with your twin flame and can more intimately unpack the lessons of the dream with this intimate aspect of yourself. Shared dreaming with another individual in any case can be impactful, however, particularly when you agree to program the dream by drawing the same agenda and preparing the same mapping.

Joining Your Guide or Mentor

As mentioned earlier, you might be joined by a dream guide or mentor at your dreamscape, particularly if you have previously visualized one and included one in your preparations. This is really not the same as a shared dream with another individual, since your guide or mentor is not sharing the dream in the same way as you but offering direction to you in your lucid dream. In this sense, this helper is more like an extra-knowledgeable assistant than an associate.

Joining a Group of Dreamers

On the other hand, you could join an entire group of people who are sharing the same dreamscape. This could be accidental or planned in advance. As a group, you could agree to draw the same agenda for your lucid dreams so that your mapping will take you to the same dreamscape with the same orientation. This could be a powerful dynamic for a group of like-minded people—perhaps a spiritual group who wants group insight from a shared area of interest.

You also could find yourself accidentally joined in a dreamscape by others who have similar interests. This could be a large group or even occasional individuals who come your way. We really should not think of this as a chance encounter or accidental in the strictest sense, however. There is no such thing as chance encounter. Instead, consider it meaningful coincidence or synchronicity, as depth psychologist Carl Jung called it. You are synchronized with these individuals and following a similar karma trail of opportunity and revelation. So we must infer that your spirit and the spirit of others are at a similar state of evolution and searching for similar insight.

Your spirits might even recognize these other individuals, even though you have no memory of them on the physical plane. What I have personally discovered and repeatedly met with are other individuals whom I did not know on this physical plane. After meeting with them randomly in dreamscapes, however, I might subsequently come to recognize them in the physical realm.

Recalling lucid dreams, where I randomly encountered strangers sharing the same dreamscape, I think my initial reaction was that they were not people I might encounter in the physical plane. But when I discovered that many of them seemed disoriented at the dreamscape, it began to occur to me that they were accidentally experiencing a vivid dream. Then I began to encounter people on the street during waking hours that seemed very familiar from my lucid dreams.

Many people have the experience in a lucid dream of visiting a sort of teaching center or room of higher learning with other people. The group seems to gather without advance social coordination. If you have not experienced this sort of vivid teaching dream or have no memory of it, you probably know someone close to you who has described it. Commonly, the group sits in a wide circle on the floor, awaiting a teacher to enter the room. The teacher enters from a side door outside the circle. The teacher seems to speak to each person present on an individual level in a personal way. Sometimes this dreamscape is called the upper room.

Ultimately a Personal Journey

The spiritual journey of personal discovery in a lucid dream is a little different from that of Odysseus, Arjuna, or even Dorothy. It is a sojourn outside known time and space in spirit consciousness. It is an interdimensional adventure outside the confines of the three dimensions of our known physical world. It does not start in Kansas or Troy and does not involve tornado-powered flight or sailing vessels. It takes us beyond the known world in an energy body that evades the gatekeepers of time and space as well as the three dimensions and linear view we have of the known world.

And this journey never ends. It takes you far from the known world into the unknown world for self-discovery and then takes you home. But lucid dreaming can be repeated again and again to take you far from your home base for future exploration. In all likelihood, we will never stop lucid dreaming once we have started dreamwork in earnest. Our recurring and continuation dreams will continue through this lifetime and probably many more, as an ultimate personal journey of spiritual exploration. The intelligent energy within you that we commonly call our inner self, our eternal flame, or our spirit has no end. It searches and grows forever. As psychologist and author Dr. Michael Newton put it, this is the journey of the soul.

CHAPTER 16

Parallel Lives Visited in Your Dreams

It also is possible to visit parallel worlds, parallel realities, and parallel lives in your lucid dreams. The concept of parallel realities is accepted more and more by many people, including cutting-edge theoretical physicists. We must always remember that our concept of reality is based on our ability to perceive and act within only three dimensions. Anything outside those three dimensions as we perceive them would be an alternate reality to us. Since dimensions are layered, let us conclude that we are caught between layers and cannot see layers above or below our surface reality.

This opens doors of speculation, then, to a multiverse theory of creation, with universes that are beyond our sensory perception and realities beyond our three-dimensional limited viewpoint. P. D. Ouspensky's description of people trapped in a second-floor apartment with no view outside or above and below shows how limited our concept of reality is. Ouspensky in *Tertium Origanum* concludes, however, that people can look beyond the closed-in box in which they find themselves through altered consciousness in meditation.

Our heightened consciousness, after all, is nonphysical energized intelligence that allows us to extend our vision beyond the limitations of the five physical senses. With heightened awareness, we can learn to see with new eyes, as discovered by all successful shamanic spirit walkers, yoga masters, psychics, remote viewers, and psyops operatives. In this real sense, we can climb out of the box and see with acute vision not dependent on five physical senses, our three-dimensional limitations, or our linear view of reality.

Interdimensional travel can be self-programmed in a lucid dream in the same way you would otherwise plan a trip to an earlier time in your life, an earlier lifetime, or a remote part of the known world. This interdimensional trip into unknown worlds can be drawn on the clear blank slate in front of your mind's eye with enough focused intent that your complete understanding of this frontier is not required. Your spirit will understand what you have intended and will follow your agenda as a perfect map with unerring accuracy.

Is it possible (Do you not agree?) that we are living parallel lives on a parallel world in a parallel reality just beyond our ability to see with physical eyes? I must ask you now whether you are ever conscious on some level of a possible dual existence. Do you ever sense that a disconnect aspect of you is living a separate life in another place, just outside your sight? Do you ever feel an awareness of a part of you that is far removed from your physical presence here but is operating in much the same sense on another plane of existence? Where might this be? Your consciousness can find the place if you draw it into your lucid-dream plans.

Another Place

Our lucid dreams, as we have discussed, can take us anywhere that we visualize with focused intent. That can be a place on the other side of the world, a mountaintop that we have only read about, or a distant land beyond the horizon. There are no limitations other than our ability to visualize with focused intent. If it exists on any plane of existence or any dimension—far or near—you can visit there in a lucid dream. Your consciousness can take you to a distant planet or a secret cave. It can take you to parallel worlds beyond any telescope or rocket ship. We are not talking, however, about imaginary worlds but real worlds beyond our limited physical perception.

We must have confidence in our inner self as energized intelligence to bring us safely to a greater sense of reality through discovery outside our physical limitations. Your eternal spirit knows where it is going and what you need to see. As your eternal guardian, it will not put you in harm's way or simply entertain you with fantasy excursions that are not real and meaningful.

Another Time

As discussed previously, time is undeniably looped as one single timeline, only part of which we normally perceive in our physical lives with our limited perception. The proof of this, perhaps, is in how many people visit their past lives in lucid dreams or have dreams of the future. This suggests that they have actually visited the past and future to personally witness events out of our normal frame of reference in the here and now.

If your visit to see yourself in the future or the past seems to put you in front of a very familiar version of yourself—one that you can readily accept as yourself—then you are undoubtedly witnessing yourself in another point along the eternal timeline. The question of identity here is whether the extension of yourself appears familiar—perhaps not even physically but energetically, mentally, and emotionally. People change over time, and particularly from one lifetime to another, but you should be able to connect with this suspected extension of you energetically and magnetically. This is karmic attraction.

On the other hand, you may sense no strong connection to this person that you have visited, suggesting that it is not you in a future or past time, but a parallel-world version of you. It might seem hard to tell the difference, but whenever you program a self-induced lucid dream to specifically visit a parallel world or parallel reality, you are likely to find a different version of yourself there. So, once again, our focused intent in drawing our dream destination will determine what you visit. What you see on the clear blank slate in front of your mind's eye is what you get.

Another Incarnation

More typically, our lucid dreams will take us to visit a continuation of ourselves in the future or the past in what we normally conceive as an incarnation of our current self. This is not the same as a parallel-world double of ourselves that would be outside our frame of reference as three-dimensional physical beings. The interdimensional double in a parallel reality might be very much like you, but not a continuation of this karmic soul.

I must say that I am often aware of a double of myself living simultaneously at this same point on the timeline but in another dimension. We were undoubtedly intended to be more than three-dimensional beings but have not yet mastered this expansive reality. So there is another version of me living out a parallel life outside this three-dimensional manifest world we occupy as physical beings. I am sometimes able to connect to this parallel life through projected thought forms as energized consciousness that will pass through all physical barriers as pure energy. The connection for me is weak.

Many people, it seems, do seem to sense a double out there somewhere. They look for this double in strange cities in crowds but, naturally, will not find their interdimensional double on this physical plane. This double lives beyond the folds of space, where our light does not reach. Yet, we look with amazement at people who resemble ourselves in crowds, as though we are nonetheless aware of a double that lives in a parallel reality and parallel world beyond our sight.

What Visiting Our Double Can Teach Us

So what could we learn by visiting our double in a parallel world? That is probably the major question that we should consider. This guidebook on self-directed lucid dreaming is not intended for entertainment, after all, but as a serious outline for how to explore programmed vivid dreams out of body for insight and growth. It is a journal of the spirit to feed the spirit and make us whole. There is so much we do not know physically in this lifetime of ours but need to understand as eternal travelers.

Many people might never think of visiting a parallel reality or parallel world or think it even possible. It is so far outside our physical frame of reference as three-dimensional creatures that perhaps it never occurs to most people. They might have a vague sense of a parallel existence that somehow touches them from time to time, but might consider that a longing to go beyond our reality or a bounce-back of thought projections that they have directed to the edge of our reality. It is hard to understand how different individuals might actually think about realities beyond what we can see and touch on a physical level.

But the first step in recognizing and reaching out is always conceiving how something else can exist. Consequently, it would be possible to visualize visiting a parallel world and parallel reality when we visualize everything we intend to experience in our lucid dream. You can be as specific or vague as you choose in drawing your agenda on the clear blank slate in front of your mind's eye. Spirit always will attempt to take you to your designated target and the specific scenario you have visualized for your lucid dream.

You can visualize yourself as an occupant in this parallel world. If you have a double in this parallel reality, spirit will certainly find the way to take you to your double. Always remember that spirit knows more than your outer self knows. This is your energized consciousness that exists throughout time and space. It knows where you have been and where you are going. If there is an interdimensional double of you that exists in another reality, your spirit likely knows that. Our consciousness is our personal connection to universal consciousness or cosmic intelligence.

So we are left with the prospect of what might logically be learned from visiting your double in a parallel reality. The question, really, is what you conceive as something to learn and how you visualize that conception in your dream planning. You must ask the right questions to get the right answers. If you do not have the questions at this point, you would not understand the answers, even if given to you.

I should think it would be valuable to ask your double in another reality to resolve basic—not personal—questions that puzzle you in this physical reality. These are the big questions that all of us ponder. Who am I in the grand scheme of things? What is the purpose of living? Where am I likely heading? How do all the pieces fit together?

There is a myriad of other big questions to ask someone just like you from a very different point of view. From where your double stands, how do things look? What, you ask, are you likely to learn in a lucid dream that is properly planned, regardless of where it takes you?

CHAPTER 17

Implications

There are always implications to everything we do and think. When we begin a journey of discovery in a lucid dream, we are both taking action and projecting conscious thought. There is the consideration of moral responsibility, but also the basic recognition that what we do and think creates consequences on many levels, including a ripple effect that extends far beyond us.

We include implications for what we think as well as what we do here, for good reason. Our thoughts have real form, as visionary authors Annie Besant and Charles Leadbeater argued. As we project our conscious thoughts outward as forms with directional impact, as suggested by Indian sage J. Krishnamurti, our conscious thoughts influence others. If you have ever walked into a room filled with angry or emotional people, then you have felt the impact of their heavy-handed thoughts bouncing off walls and people within range. You must then assume responsibility for your projected conscious thought forms as intelligent energy you have directed intentionally or unintentionally.

When we program a self-directed lucid dream with the intent to leave the physical body with our energized consciousness, we must assume responsibility both for our actions and our thoughts. Our subtle energy bodies are carried with focused and projected thought forms with a destination and purpose in mind.

Implications for the actions and thoughts that we direct in our lucid dreams are a factor in any programmed dreams of discovery described in this book. We will focus here specifically on the implications of our actions and thoughts in a lucid dream into a parallel world and parallel reality.

Realize up front that we are probably intruders to this alternate realm. At the very least, we should consider ourselves to be interlopers who do not normally reside or function there. It is an alien environment that we have penetrated. In all likelihood, our intentions for visiting were noble, as part of our ongoing journey of discovery. We go as silent observers without interacting in a lucid dream. But we have introduced a foreign element into that environment and must consider the impact and possible implications.

The softer we walk upon this environment, the better. As in other lucid dreams—but even more so here—we should touch nothing, say nothing, and project no energy at this site. We should treat it, as with all dreamscapes, as more than a dream but as a real site that should be protected and not spoiled. In such an exotic realm, we should be like a fly on the wall—a fly with a hundred eyes.

If you see what you consider to be your double in a parallel world, do not assume that you are karmically linked or in any way related. This is not a future extension of you or a past incarnation. You are not sliding on your own eternal timeline to another point in your life and that of your known world. This could be a totally different life and a totally different world outside your frame of reference. You bear only a resemblance and similarity to this alternate reality. But it is not your world or your life in any sense that is immanently personal.

Your mere presence if observed could cause a ripple effect. Anything you touch or impact could cause such an effect. The ultimate impact and range of this ripple are hard to predict, since the ripple itself collects things along the way within its wake. Think of a ripple as a small current in a stream that touches many things along its path, its energy impacting other things along the way.

If the exotic location of your remote lucid dream is not in a parallel world or reality but actually in your past or future, then the possible consequences from having an impact on the environment you visit have even-greater implications. You have a natural connection to this life and this realm. You are energetically linked to this world and this reality. Your electromagnetic energy in the form of projected consciousness is synchronized with the energy of this environment like a natural extension of you.

You cannot in any sense tamper with your own past or own future. You are there to observe and learn. As with shamanic dream walkers who visit their ancestors or look into what the future holds for their people, your out-of-body dreamwork should provide you with insight to guide you in your present lifetime, not course-correct how you see your life in the past or future.

That sort of intervention could cause a severe ripple effect in your own past or future, as you alter events or thought patterns that spill over. It is impossible to predict the direction and broad swath of such spillage, but it starts with the past or future version of you and extends into all directions from that point in the eternal timeline.

Yes, it might ultimately impact you in your current physical life, but not without carrying many things in its wake. This ripple can go in different directions that cannot be predicted, as it bounces off things and combines with other elements. It creates a life course of its own, sweeping things along with it.

So we must make every effort to confine ourselves in a lucid dream so that we do not change the course of things by our interference in the scenes we observe. This becomes a disciplined trip in which we must focus on controlling our thoughts, attention, emotional and mental impact, impression on a scene, and every movement.

Now, if you are still at this point having trouble realizing yourself out of body at your self-selected designation, then none of the following implications have much meaning for you. If you have not gone from the ability to conceive to the stages of achieving and believing in your creative visualization, then you need to start rereading this book. In no way are we describing idle dreams that occur only inside your mind as flights of imagination.

If you *do* actually reach an out-of-body dreamscape but still have doubts that you are witnessing anything that is more than idle imagination inside your mind, then you will not respect the scene that you have entered and could pollute it with your interaction. Our actions within a lucid dream always have implications. That said, the following concerns are incumbent upon us when we arrive at an out-of-body dreamscape to avoid implications that might result from our presence there.

Controlling Our Thoughts

Our consciousness that is present at a lucid dream is always able to project conscious thought forms intentionally or unintentionally. We assume that a person in a lucid dreamscape will not purposefully project a thought form, but it is also embarrassingly easy to let a thought form leak into the environment. And while you cannot interfere with a scene in the past, future, or parallel dimension by moving your arms and legs and shouting aloud, due to your lack of a physical presence there, you can nonetheless interfere with the scene by sending or leaking thought forms.

This can be hard to control, so you must be ever vigilant and disciplined as a quiet observer in your lucid dream. There is really no way to place a lid on your thoughts or govern them. You simply need to *avoid* thoughts that can be expressed in any way.

It might help to always remember in a lucid dream that you are there only to observe and not interact. You do not need to have thoughts. You only need to see with new eyes and hear with new ears to bring insight back from the dreamscape experience. Consequently, you have no need to evaluate, comment, or process any thought about what you see when at the dreamscape. You just absorb. Think of a sponge. Be that sponge.

Controlling Our Attention

So you are quietly observing what you see with your new eyes and ears at a lucid dreamscape, left with only your acute awareness that replaces what we commonly call perception and concentration in our physical mind. Now the challenge becomes to control your attention so that your acute awareness is focused only on what you see as a quiet, nonobtrusive observer. You cannot allow your acute awareness to wander. You must maintain focus only on what you have come to observe.

Wandering attention can prove dangerous, putting you in places you have not planned to be. When we wander, we can become lost and confused. We can counteract that by maintaining disciplined focus as observers. Wandering attention can put you in situations that can prove perplexing, due to your lack of prior planning. You have come with a clear agenda of what you want to observe, down to the precise scene, time, place, and characters. This is because you have a goal in mind about what you want to observe, in hopes of winning insight into something very specific and meaningful to you on a deep spiritual level. Do not deviate from what you have programmed yourself to observe.

Controlling Our Emotional and Mental Impact

Care should be taken not to let your emotional and mental subtle bodies spill over onto the scene during your programmed visit in the lucid dream. Keep in mind that the best lucid dreams take all of your subtle energy bodies along, leaving only your dense, physical body behind in peaceful repose. Your energized intelligence resides on all levels of your being, from your highest spiritual bodies to your causal body, mental body, and emotional body. When we typically leave the physical body in subtle energy bodies, our emotional and mental bodies lead the way.

Additionally, our emotional and mental bodies connect us energetically to the emotional and mental planes of existence. It would be difficult to relate to many dreamscapes without a connection to the mental and emotional planes in that reality. That is true, of course, of all planes of reality and our corresponding subtle energy bodies that connect us to those planes.

That said, it is also possible to ride our emotional energy body to a pure emotional plane, and our mental energy body to a pure mental plane of reality. That is our special connection, with each subtle energy body we possess filled with conscious energy.

But once we arrive at the dreamscape of our choosing, we also must hold our emotional energy and mental energy in check. That would be true of the energy of our other subtle energy bodies as well. We are not there to interact or even share. We are there only to observe as perfect silent witnesses. The silent witness slips quietly home with treasures found. Our treasures are insights from what we learn.

Controlling Our Impression on a Scene

Having managed to control our thoughts, attention, and emotional and mental energy in our lucid dream, we are nonetheless left with a possible impression of what we are witnessing. So we are left with how to control our impressions so they do not manifest themselves into something that can project onto a scene before us. This is tricky. The watchword here is detachment. We must stay detached as objective observers in our own dreams so that we exhibit no sort of impression from having witnessed what is before us. We just take in everything without processing the information. Spirit knows what it has seen. It doesn't need to sort it out, analyze what it has observed, or reflect upon it. It sees, understands, and knows.

This is the difference between intuitive knowledge of a spirit nature, as in gnosis, and simply knowing a little about something intellectually. Your spirit knows on a deep and profound level whatever it has observed. And it will always remember it accurately.

We must acknowledge, too, that any observer by mere presence can change a scene. It is difficult to take a photograph without really putting yourself into the picture. Visiting a dreamscape in an energy body as pure consciousness, we do not necessarily have traction on the scene. We have no pull and create no friction if we carefully avoid interaction in our spirit body. This is the goal of the perfect witness during a lucid dream of discovery.

Controlling Our Actions

You might not think that actions are even possible in a subtle energy body during a lucid dream out of body. You have no physical legs or arms, it must be said. You cannot grab someone, write something, or block a bullet. What you have is simply an etheric double augmented with an emotional body, mental body, causal body, and higher spiritual bodies of pure energy.

Some people who are practiced in out-of-body adventures, however, become more highly evolved as significant energy forms than others. There are random reports of bilocation in which the subtle energy body assumes seemingly physical characteristics outside the physical body. These people apparently find a way to carry on conversations and interact, as though whole with physicality. Perhaps it is possible in deepest meditation to visualize something material becoming invisible and relocated. Some of the more advanced sutras in raja-yoga suggest that the material can be made to disappear from this material reality through intensely focused visualization exercises.

For the rest of us—the vast majority of spirit travelers—there is no sense of form out of body, and little chance of acting in the same way a physical form would allow. Nonetheless, we hasten to add that some actions are formless but filled with impact. Herein, we repeat the familiar phrase "Do no harm." In fact, do nothing. Just observe.

Any action that you undertake could interfere with the natural flow of events in that scene, with possible implications far beyond our ability to foresee. Stay a neutral observer without action of any sort.

Controlling Our Movement

Try not to move about in your lucid dream once you reach your self-directed dreamscape. You might think it odd to worry about restricting your movement in a lucid dream out of body if you have no legs or arms as energy bodies there. You might wonder how you could have any mobility. In fact, though, you have an enhanced sense of mobility outside the physical form as boundless energy.

In an energy body, you can freely move anywhere throughout time and space without the common restrictions of the physical world. You are not restricted to only three dimensions. You do not follow any linear path. You are working with new eyes, ears, and creative intuition that allow you to instantly go to anything you are able to see with your new eyes of enhanced awareness. You see something and find yourself there. You intuit something and find yourself there. There are no clumsy physical barriers.

On the other hand, this enhanced mobility in a spirit body presents a problem at the same time. Once at a dreamscape, you will be quietly observing characters in a scene that you have programmed. It is real. Your bouncing around as restless spirit could impact the scene energetically. Your energy can be felt. It is wise to remain steadfast in one place during your visit to the dreamscape, so that your energy does not bounce all over the scene and the characters. Energy buildup can be felt by others. I am certain that you have experienced that on occasions even in the physical world, when people around you became emotionally or mentally energized.

Controlling Our Connection

Controlling our connection to the characters and events of a dreamscape we visit out of body might be most difficult, since we are there to take in everything. But taking things in as observers does not mean that we are involved. Still, it must be argued logically that we are making a connection. The best that we can hope to do, perhaps, is to make that connection weak and undetectable. The real point here is that you do not want to permit characters to sense your presence or the scene you share with them or absorb your energy, if you can avoid it.

We can minimize our connection by dissolving any sense of personal identification. We can view the scene objectively and not subjectively. Remember that there is no whole "you" in this dreamscape, in the sense that you commonly recognize as your outer self. There is only the inner self in pure energy form as a ghostlike spirit that can hide anywhere, including inside you.

Our spirit carries no psychological baggage or baffling questions but is a wide-eyed learner who absorbs new information like a sponge. It is like the child who can listen to a foreign language and then recite it, because it is not preoccupied and filled with doubt.

So we go into a dreamscape like a child without preconception and doubt, eyes wide open and taking everything in like a sponge. The child does not control the scene of knowledge or make connections. The child quickly learns with a sense of detachment, ready to absorb and grow in insight.

Now, it is not sufficient simply to read and think about all these implications and precautions here, since you are currently analyzing this information in your physical mind, which will be sleeping during your lucid dream. You now need to meditate on these implications and what precautions you need to take once at your dreamscape, so that this vital information becomes internalized within you at the deepest level of your consciousness.

CHAPTER 18
Cautions and Concerns

In addition to the preceding chapter's list of possible implications regarding one's presence in a lucid-dream site, we should also outline other possible precautions. These possibilities should not overly worry you since a lucid dream is really quite safe and painless all the way around. That is particularly true when you program a self-directed lucid dream with creative visualization and focused intent.

A dream tutorial such as this book portends to be, nonetheless, would be poorly constructed and incomplete without inclusion of all things to consider in planning your lucid dream. With that in mind, I simply want to point out little possible concerns in the process of setting up your own vivid dream of self-discovery.

Make Certain You Are Not Disrupted during Your Dream

We began this guidebook to lucid dreaming by setting the stage with a quiet and secure place for you to recline during your out-of-body dream. There is some worry about disturbances in the room where you sleep that should be clarified here. The ability to seamlessly leave the physical body during a lucid dream depends on the physical mind's sense of security and peacefulness. It must agree to allow the hidden higher consciousness of the inner self to assume leadership while it rests. It must have assurance that your physical body—which is its overarching concern—is safe during this period. There will be no usual watchdog.

Startling the physical body during a lucid dream, then, could trouble the physical mind to the point where it distrusts the process and will not harmoniously concede control to the heightened consciousness in dreams. That distrust could be lasting, as you continue your adventures into lucid dreaming.

Little can happen in self-programming a lucid dream when the physical mind senses danger and stays on guard. The mind then resumes its normal function as gatekeeper, with primary focus on safeguarding your physical body.

Make Certain You Are Physically Comfortable

That said, you must reassure yourself physically before entering a lucid dream that the body will be comfortable during the entire process. This includes wearing loose-fitting, comfortable clothing, with shoes and jewelry removed and high collars unbuttoned for maximum comfort level. A sense of physical discomfort can quickly return you to your physical body and out of heightened consciousness. You do not want to suddenly become aware of your feet swelling or your body sweating during a lucid dream, since you will quickly return to your physical body or find it difficult to leave your physical body whatsoever. You do not want to suddenly become uncomfortably aware of a clothing wrinkle under your back that irritates you where you recline.

If you go slowly in setting up your lucid dream, you will allow space to make certain that you are physically comfortable before you attempt to leave the physical body. You have all the time in the world. Time is meaningless. You are becoming an eternal time traveler on a journey of self-discovery.

Make Certain You Are Totally at Rest

Take plenty of time to make certain that your entire physical body is totally at rest and entering a sleep mode of numbness before you continue setting up your lucid dream. You cannot leave your physical body behind for even the briefest lucid-dream adventure if your physical body still feels alert and awake.

Trying to leave before your physical body is totally to sleep can prove frustrating and futile. That is particularly true for a waking dream outside normal sleep mode. Most likely, you will find it impossible to leave on your lucid dream. If you start to leave, you could snap back into your body. Consequently, you need to put the physical side of you fully to rest.

So I suggest focusing strategically on each part of your physical body, starting at your toes, to command your physical body to become heavy, tired, numb, and sleeping. I do not move my attention to another part of the body until I feel nothing in the body part that I have started to put to sleep. When the toes become numb and heavy, then I should feel nothing in the toes. I next move my attention to the legs. I put the lower legs to sleep before moving to the upper thighs. Then I focus on putting the abdomen to sleep, followed gradually by the chest, arms, throat, and face. When I sense no feeling in my ears, I include focus on the top of my head to put even any feeling in my hair to sleep.

This cannot and should not be hurried if you want to put the physical body to rest, as you must.

Make Certain to Put the Mind to Rest

It would be a mistake to stop our effort to put the physical self to rest by stopping at the ears and hair. Next, you must make extra certain that your physical mind is also at rest. Many people make the mistake in believing that they need their mind to continue, overlooking the superconscious mind of the inner self. Or they think that the mind is more than the brain and are approaching something commonly called mindfulness by quietly reflecting that this is still the analytical brain or physical brain in charge. We are not focused here on putting the mind in cooperation with the body for a sort of body-awareness or mind-body conjunction. We are looking beyond both the physical body and the mind. We are looking totally beyond the physical plane.

We need to take our brain offline to allow the pure consciousness of our energy body to operate outside normal parameters. Until you have put the mind to rest with a sense of comfort and tranquility, you cannot expect your higher consciousness to spring forward to take you beyond the physical realm in a lucid dream of discovery.

The only way to "slay" the mind, as yoga meditation sometimes suggests, is to actually work in harmony with the mind by convincing it to let its guard down. It will do so only once it is assured that the body is safe and secure and the mind is not needed for a period of peaceful rest.

If you cannot reach this agreement with your physical mind, then you will not be able to actually leave the body, since your mind will hold you fast in place. You might imagine that you are going to a programmed dreamscape, but you are only approaching a space inside your physical mind and not actually leaving the physical plane. Reaching inner harmony on a total level of your whole being is not easy or quick but is absolutely essential in overcoming the limitations of time and space.

You should sense the increased presence of a superconscious mind that has replaced your analytical, physical brain. This heightened consciousness is now fully awake and alive and will direct you in states of your lucid dreaming. At this stage, you should sense a heightened presence with a consciousness that is racing at an accelerated speed.

Make Certain Your Physical Senses Are Blocked

One thing that will keep you inside your physical body and unable to proceed in a conscious energy body outside time and space is a lingering connection to your five physical senses. Your sense of hearing, seeing, smell, taste, and touch are your touchstones that connect you to your immediate physical environment.

It is possible to put our physical body to sleep from head to toe, put the physical mind to rest, and still have one toe in the physical plane, which prevents you from leaving your body behind in a lucid dream. You might be vaguely aware of a slight scent, sound, or touch where you recline. That will be enough to keep you grounded and prevent you from totally shutting down your physical body and mind to enter heightened consciousness.

I always remember the Indian sage J. Krishnamurti commenting how a group of older men he knew found it hard to meditate with the sound of children playing. They should have been able to tune out their hearing. It is assumed these men selected a quiet, somewhat secluded place to meditate but were nonetheless distracted by the slightest sound nearby.

Tuning out our physical senses requires discipline. It requires focus and will. It is not always easy but always essential to entering a state of heightened consciousness. Consequently, people should not proceed with setting up a lucid dream until all sensory input from the physical world around them is muted. This should be part of putting the physical body to rest. It should be clear in reaching a state of inner harmony as a whole being that the brain is safely limited to automatic maintenance in keeping the blood flowing, lungs breathing, and other essential functions operating to keep the physical body safe.

We do not need to smell incense, essential oils, or lovely flowers during this period when we are asking our inner consciousness to rise above the physical plane in a state of heightened awareness out of body. Such sensations only allow the physical mind to continue processing information and operating fully.

Scented candles, incense, and essential oils might be popular for setting up a sort of meditative state of quiet reflection inside the body but are not helpful to our goal here. These sensory triggers will hold you back from leaving the body and totally shutting off the physical mind. The same could be said for other popular meditation aids such as sound as inducement. You cannot keep one toe in the water and hope to go beyond your current environment.

If you still believe that such inducements will allow you to go into a deeper state of mind, you are more accurately contemplating mind control and controlled hypnotic states of subconsciousness. This is what we see typically in a so-called guided meditation. We want to go beyond that to a state of superconsciousness by shutting down the mind and allowing the inner superconscious mind to come forward on its own without interference.

Make Certain You See the Blank Slate

Another factor that will keep you from setting up an out-of-body lucid dream is a failure to find the clear blank slate in front of your mind's eye. You must not proceed until you see and sense nothing but this clear blank slate on which to visualize your agenda, since this will become your map to take you to your designated dreamscape outside the physical realm.

Your superconsciousness, now in control, should seamlessly make this happen for you, since you are no longer encumbered by your physical brain to analyze the situation and screen your every thought and action. Rest assured that your inner heightened consciousness should allow you to proceed at this point.

Some people might visualize a blackboard, while others visualize a whiteboard. The idea that is most important is that you see a clear blank slate and nothing else. It might take some time and effort for you to visualize this slate, but it is essential that you do.

Our technique here is to draw pictures on the board in front of your mind's eye and avoid thoughts, words, memories, or sensations that bring you back into your physical mind. Once you have crossed beyond the mind as gatekeeper, you do not want to linger at the gate for one last look at the other side.

Make Certain That You Are Harmonically Synchronized

We are not trying to change who you are or deny your physical nature here. We are only trying to reach an inner harmony of the wholeness of who you truly are. You are more than your physical self. The inner self and your hidden superconsciousness should be allowed to come forward prominently and unhindered on occasion.

So your meditation in setting up a self-programmed lucid dream becomes a deep and active meditation that must totally shut down the physical side of your whole being to allow the inner self to fully emerge. You will know that you have achieved this level of deep meditation when you cease to process thoughts in the normal sense and see only inside yourself.

In reaching total harmony, you will sense a vibrational level of radiance and bliss that you could never achieve physically. You will feel warm, tingly, and tranquil. This is the place of inner peace and bliss that few people ever really experience, distracted as we are by the lovely smell of flowers, gentle breezes, and happy memories that otherwise preoccupy our attention on a purely physical level.

If you are unable to reach this holistic harmony so that your physical mind willingly allows the inner consciousness to take control for your lucid dream outside mundane time and space, then you need to work on achieving this total harmony or you will not be able to leave your body.

Make Certain You Have Provided the Trigger to Leave

If you have successfully achieved inner harmony where your mind gives way to your consciousness, and you have visualized what you want to do and where you want to go in your dream, then you still require a sort of trigger to leave. Think of it as a starting gun to send you on your way.

If you have not prepared a proper cue to trigger your departure into your dreamscape, you will not leave your physical body to experience the exciting lucid dream that you have programmed for yourself. So you need a prompt that tells when you are ready to leave. Otherwise, you will just be reclining comfortably with a frustrating desire for what you want to explore.

Personally, I prefer a sort of posthypnotic trigger where I postpone bringing the map before my mind's eye. That allows me to prepare myself for an immediate departure as soon as I bring the map forward. That is why I prefer to tuck the slate where I have drawn what I want to explore, and where I want to go into the back of my consciousness to set up the prompt to leave. Once the slate is tucked away, I tell myself that I will automatically and instantaneously leave my body to visit my dreamscape outside the body as soon as the slate is recalled before my mind's eye. When it is recalled, my mind's eye recognizes it as the trigger to leave the physical body to go where I have visualized anywhere outside normal time and space. Nothing holds me back once I have received the prompt to leave.

Make Certain You Are Properly Oriented at Your Dreamscape

It sounds repetitive to review what you should do upon arrival at your designed lucid-dream site, but it is most important to follow precise procedures to experience the dream experience fully and safely. If you do not properly orient yourself upon arrival, you will not have a sense of reality and will find it difficult to benefit much from the experience. There is also the fear that you will plant yourself into the scene as an active participant and not a quiet observer that does not change the flow of events.

Consequently, I encourage you to take special caution to properly orient yourself as soon as you find yourself in a lucid-dream site. Do this by satisfying yourself that you are truly present and truly able to observe quietly and unobtrusively as the perfect witness. You are there only to observe and learn.

Make Certain You Understand When to Leave

A concern that many individuals seem to have about out-of-body experiences in a lucid dream is that you can safely and efficiently leave the physical body and return at will, without problems. This suggests a confidence problem, which erodes over time with experience.

It helps here to understand exactly when you can leave the dream site to return to the physical body. You need to internalize the knowledge that you will automatically and seamlessly return from the dreamscape just as soon as you have learned everything that you visualized on your slate as your agenda. If you do not learn everything that you hoped to learn, then you will leave as soon as you have exhausted the agenda that you have programmed. It is important to recognize that we cannot hope to learn everything that concerns our inner spirit in one lucid dream, but we can fully explore an agenda that we have drawn for the experience.

Hold the Dream inside You When You Return

It is easy to return from a vivid, lucid dream with high energy and want to bound out of bed. That is a mistake. You should take time upon returning to your physical body to hold the dream in your consciousness to review, to meditate on the dream without analyzing it. This allows your higher consciousness to internalize the message and imprint it on the spirit.

To totally own the dream and enrich the spirit with the lessons learned, you should allow a few minutes upon reentry to the body for your higher consciousness to review the dream before your physical mind assumes control. Your inner spirit has great awareness but can profit perhaps from allowing the scene that you have just witnessed in the lucid dream to replay in front of your mind's eye. Use that same blank slate before your mind's eye, but now like a movie screen.

If you do not do that, the impression of your out-of-body experience might not be clearly imprinted on your consciousness but appear as fragments of information. Leave nothing to doubt here. Review the dream until you sense that you have captured it. Then take a few more minutes to remain still and quiet while you meditate on it. This does not mean analysis, but an opportunity for your inner spirit to fully process the dream experience. This is not a deep or active meditation, but a period of gentle reflection. The spirit within you can absorb the message to process in its own way. Avoid concentration or attempting to analyze the dream. Just let it flow within you.

Provide for an Easy Return for Continuation Dreams

You will likely want to return to the same dream again and again to fully explore matters of great concern to you on a deep level. You can draw everything you want to experience in a lucid dream with great depth upon your clear blank slate and still find a need to return to the same dreamscape for further exploration.

Consequently, you need the understanding and assurance that you can program essentially the same dreamscape again to return to the same basic time, place, and circumstances to continue your experience. This is a learning exercise for the enrichment of your eternal spirit, after all, and well worth the extra effort to fully explore areas of greatest concern. It might require many out-of-body trips to begin to really understand the hidden meaning that you seek through this exploration.

If you do not have the confidence that you can return to a specific dreamscape for further instruction, you might not be able to fully process the information that you have retrieved for your conscious spirit. It is, therefore, important to recognize that you can easily program the same dream again and again, perhaps adding to the agenda that you carefully draw upon your clear blank slate.

CHAPTER 19

Exercises That Program Intentions, Guides, and Shared Dreams

We have described various exercises throughout this guidebook to walk you through the things you need to do and know in programming a self-directed lucid dream. These include drawing pictures before your mind's eye to creatively visualize your intent, summoning a dream guide, and self-directing a lucid dream outside the physical body beyond mundane time and space.

We will now walk you step by step through some select exercises to program intentions, guides, and shared dreams so that they are clear in your mind. It is important to understand the sequencing of programming your own self-directed lucid dream so that you can learn to do it yourself. This is not guided meditation. This is self-directed meditation to focus intent, get in touch with your inner self, creatively visualize where and what you want to experience in a vivid dream, and seamlessly leave the physical body and return from a real experience outside our three dimensions with purpose and meaning.

It is important that you develop a comfort level with these steps within you, so that you are not holding the book in your hands to read and analyze with your physical eyes and mind while programming a dream. You should read and absorb the steps now so that they come to you easily in setting up your own self-directed lucid dream in an altered state of consciousness. An option to beginning this process would be to have someone softly read to initially guide you through these steps, although I really think it better for you to do this totally on your own when ready in a quiet, private room.

EXERCISE 1:

Drawing Your Intentions for a Self-Directed Lucid Dream

NEEDED:
- quiet, secluded room or place to meditate comfortably in peace
- bed, pad, or blanket on which to recline, with arms and legs outstretched, or else a straight-back chair to sit on, with bare feet firmly grounded (no part of the body should be crossed, to allow energy to flow freely)
- loose-fitting clothing, with shoes and jewelry removed

Procedure

1. Become still and quiet, visualizing putting your physical body to sleep. Focus on your feet and tell them to become heavy, tired, and numb until they go to sleep. Then focus the same way on your lower legs and then your upper body. Work your way up the body through the torso, chest, arms, throat, and head until you have successfully put even your ears and hairs on top of your head to sleep without any feeling.
2. Begin controlled, rhythmic breathing with deep breaths that you hold inside you before consciously expelling. Take about three seconds to inhale oxygen, with appreciation, and then hold it deep within you for about three seconds, conscious of the energy in that air. Then slowly expel this air with a blessing. Continue this rhythmic, deep breathing until it becomes automatic and a part of you.
3. Close your eyes and tune out all external and internal distractions, including thoughts going through your mind and sensory perception of sounds, sights, smells, feels, and tastes of the physical world around you. You should eventually see nothing but darkness inside you, with no words, sounds, or impressions.
4. You should establish a sense of total body harmony and sense of comfort by assuring your physical mind that it will be safe and rested during a period of sleep. During this time, your mind willingly allows your higher consciousness to emerge from deep inside you. Your mind will continue to keep the physical body's autonomic system functioning during this peaceful period of physical rest, but nothing more.
5. In the darkness, your inner consciousness begins to focus on a clear blank slate before you. There is nothing on this slate.

Exercises That Program Intentions, Guides, and Shared Dreams 141

6. You begin to visualize images of what you want to see and experience in your lucid dream of discovery with focused intent. Do not write with words or thoughts but only draw or paint pictures of where and when you want to go in your dream and what you want to learn. You can include characters, a scene, a scenario . . . it can be anywhere you like in the known world or outside the known world. It can even be outside known time and space. This will be an adventure of consciousness as pure intelligent energy without physical restrictions. It can extend beyond our physically known three dimensions. (As an option, you can allow the spirit inside you to totally determine where it senses you need to go and what you need to learn in your dream, and allow spirit to draw the agenda upon the clear blank slate. In any case, it is still your higher consciousness and inner self who will determine your agenda.) Focusing your conscious awareness on what you visualize on the clear blank slate with deliberation allows you more opportunity to fully internalize where you will be going in your dream.
7. When you sense that you have painted a picture of where you want to go and what you want to see, then briefly tuck that slate into the back of your consciousness, to recall later. When you recall it, you will automatically and instantaneously depart your physical body to your designated dreamscape, using that slate as an unerring map to guide you.
8. Now in the darkness, prepare yourself to leave your body, with the awareness that your physical self will be safe and rested during your lucid dream. (If you are programming a lucid dream to occur during normal sleep time and not a waking dream, then you could skip the next step. You can give your consciousness the posthypnotic command upon entering regular sleep, to automatically recall your drawn tablet as the agenda to follow as a perfect map.)
9. To program a waking dream, recall the slate that you have prepared as your agenda once you are prepared to leave your physical body to the designation of your lucid dream. You should automatically leave the physical body in a consciousness energy body that takes you instantly to the site you have programmed.
10. Once you arrive at your designated dreamscape, immediately orient yourself. Satisfy yourself that you are truly present and that you are really witnessing the situation you programmed. Do not project or put yourself into the scene in any way, but quietly observe while remaining still and focused with your acute awareness in your conscious energy body.

11. When you sense that you have observed everything that you intended to learn in this dreamscape or have addressed everything on your programmed agenda, then you should instantaneously return to your physical body.
12. When back in your physical body, do not stir or open your eyes at first. Do not begin thinking. Instead, allow yourself some time for your inner self to relive the dream you have just experienced so that your inner self has full recall and clarity. Do not attempt to analyze or think about the dream, but simply focus on it in detailed outline.
13. Then allow your consciousness a little time to meditate on the dream to absorb it and process it internally. Again, this should not involve mental analysis.
14. Now you can open your eyes and slowly allow sensation to return to your physical body before carefully moving. Take some time to do this slowly and gently. You have had a great adventure and traveled far and wide.
15. You might opt to record your lucid dream in outline form in a dream dictionary. There is no need to try to analyze it, and your physical mind would be ill equipped to do that anyway. Simply record the basic flow of the dream and add to it whenever you program a continuation of this same basic dream.

EXERCISE 2:
Summoning a Dream Guide

NEEDED:
- quiet, secluded room or space that is safe for private meditation
- bed, pad, or blanket on which to recline, with arms and legs outstretched, or else a straight-back chair to sit on, with bare feet firmly grounded (do not cross any part of your body, to allow energy to flow freely)
- loose-fitting clothing, with shoes and any jewelry removed

Procedure

1. Become still and quiet, focused on putting your physical body to sleep. First focus on your feet and tell them to become heavy, tired, and numb until they go to sleep. Then focus in the same way on your lower legs and then upper thighs. Work your way up the body through the torso,

chest, arms, throat, and head until you have successfully put even your ears and the hairs on top of your head to sleep without any feeling.
2. Begin controlled, rhythmic breathing with deep breaths that you hold inside you before consciously expelling. Take about three seconds to inhale, with appreciation, and then hold it deep within you for approximately three seconds, conscious of the energy in that oxygen. Then slowly expel this air for about three seconds with a blessing. Continue this rhythmic, deep breathing until it becomes automatic and becomes a part of you.
3. Close your eyes and tune out all external and internal distractions, including thoughts going through your mind and sensory perception of sounds, sights, smells, feels, and tastes of the physical world around you. You should eventually see nothing but darkness inside you, with no words, sounds, or impressions.
4. You should establish a sense of total body harmony and sense of comfort by assuring your physical mind that it will be safe and rested during a period of sleep. During this time, your mind willingly allows your higher consciousness to emerge from deep inside you. Your mind will continue to keep the physical body's autonomic system functioning during this peaceful period of physical rest, but nothing more.
5. In the darkness, your inner consciousness begins to focus on a clear blank slate before you. There is nothing on this slate. You begin to visualize a picture of the sort of dream guide you want to help you. You will visualize this guide exactly as you expect him or her to be. Do not write with words or thoughts but only draw or paint pictures. It does not matter how precisely you produce your picture of this dream guide. It only matters that you employ the inherent power of your conscious thought forms and direct it onto the clear tablet in front of you. Your thought forms will go out into the great expanse to find your dream guide like a magnet seeking its missing magnetic pole. If what you draw has meaning and importance to you on a deep level, then it will be sufficient.
6. Now tuck that picture into the back of your consciousness, to recall and project as a summons when you are ready. In the new darkness inside you, prepare to project that creative thought form that you have drawn into the great expanse beyond you. You should have the confidence that when you do so, it will reach its mark with unerring accuracy like one end of a magnet drawn positively to the other end.
7. Now recall the images you have drawn. When you do so, it should automatically and instantaneously leave your body to its mark.

8. NOTE: Depending on how you visualize your picture and the intent that you put into it, the dream guide that you summon could appear automatically in virtually every lucid dream that you plan. On the other hand, you might want to include the dream mentor in what you draw for each lucid dream, adding the guide to when and where you want to go and what you want to experience. Your dream guide might offer an introduction or might just suddenly appear. Each guide is different. Your guide could be formal, funny, tutorial, or collegial. Treat your guide well with respect, courtesy, and attention.

EXERCISE 3:
Program Shared Dreams

There are options for how to share a lucid dream with a dream companion. We will briefly outline the steps to program a shared dream so that you can visit a dreamscape together and perhaps discuss it later with your companion as a common learning experience. You could begin by setting up the dream together in the same room or coordinate your dream from separate locations. The shared dream could be with another individual or even with a group that coordinates their dreamwork. Note that some shared dreams might prove easier than others. Shared dreaming is hardly essential for your dreamwork, but you might find it beneficial to you and your special companions. First we will outline a self-directed dream that you share with a friend who enters your shared dream from a physical remote location.

Prior Arrangement

Before programming your lucid dream, you need to coordinate with your intended dream companion just where and when you plan to go in your out-of-body dream, with as much detail as possible. You should determine a time when both of you will begin setting up your shared lucid dream, so that you can enter the dreamscape at the same time.

NEEDED:
- quiet, secluded room or space that is safe for private meditation
- bed, pad, or blanket on which to recline, with arms and legs outstretched, or else a straight-back chair to sit on, with bare feet firmly grounded (do not cross any part of your body, to allow energy to flow freely)
- loose-fitting clothing, with shoes and any jewelry removed

Procedure

1. Become still and quiet, visualizing putting your physical body to sleep. Focus on your feet first and tell them to become heavy, tired, and numb until they go to sleep. Then focus in the same way on your lower legs and then upper body. Work your way up the body through the torso, chest, arms, throat, and head until you have successfully put even your ears and hairs on top of your head to sleep, without any feeling.
2. Begin controlled, rhythmic breathing with deep breaths that you hold inside you before consciously expelling. Take about three seconds to inhale, with appreciation, and then hold it deep within you for about three seconds, conscious of the energy in that oxygen. Then slowly expel this air with a blessing. Continue this rhythmic, deep breathing until it becomes automatic and becomes a part of you.
3. Close your eyes and tune out all external and internal distractions, including thoughts going through your mind and sensory perception of sounds, sights, smells, feels, and tastes of the physical world around you. You should eventually see nothing but darkness inside you, with no words, sounds, or impressions.
4. You should establish a sense of total body harmony and sense of comfort by assuring your physical mind that it will be safe and rested during a period of sleep. During this time, your mind willingly allows your higher consciousness to emerge from deep inside you. Your mind will continue to keep the physical body's autonomic system functioning during this peaceful period of physical rest, but nothing more.
5. In the darkness, your inner consciousness begins to visualize a clear blank slate before you. There is nothing on this slate. You begin to draw a composite picture of what and where you have decided to meet your friend and under what circumstances. Be certain that you include your dream companion in what you draw, with the intent to join your companion at this dreamscape.
6. When you sense that you have painted a picture of where you want to go and what you want to see, briefly tuck that slate into the back of your consciousness, to recall later. When you recall it, you will automatically and instantaneously depart your physical body to your designated dreamscape, using that slate as an unerring map to guide you.
7. In the darkness, prepare yourself to leave your body, with the awareness that your physical self will be safe and rested during your lucid dream.

8. Now tuck away the image you have drawn, to call forward when ready to leave. When you do so, it should provide a prompt for you to automatically and instantaneously leave your body to reach its destination.
9. Now recall the slate that you have prepared as your agenda once you are prepared to leave your physical body to the designation of your lucid dream. You should automatically leave the physical body in a consciousness energy body that takes you instantly to the site you have programmed.
10. Once you arrive at your designated dreamscape, immediately orient yourself. Satisfy yourself that you are truly present and that you are really witnessing the situation you programmed. You should also be aware of your dream companion there, although you might not see your companion. Still, you can sense the other's presence. Do not interact or acknowledge your dream companion or anyone else in the dreamscape. Do not project or put yourself into the scene in any way, but quietly observe while remaining still and focused with your acute awareness in a conscious energy body. (It is possible that you have arrived before your dream companion and might consider waiting. In any event, the two of you have programmed the same lucid dream and can both experience it, even if you do not connect at the dreamscape.)
11. When you sense that you have observed everything that you intended to learn in this dreamscape, you should instantaneously return to your physical body.
12. When back in your physical body, do not stir or open your eyes at first. Do not begin thinking. Instead, allow yourself some time for your inner self to relive the dream you have just experienced, so that it has full recall and clarity. Do not attempt to analyze or think about the dream, but simply focus on it in detail.
13. Allow your consciousness a little time to meditate on the dream to absorb it and process it internally. Again, this should not involve mental analysis. Subsequently, you can confer with your dream companion to share observations and insights gleaned from the shared dream.

EXERCISE 4:
Starting with a Dream Companion in the Same Room

1. I can personally attest that a shared dream where both of you start by reclining in the same room can be most profound. This is particularly true if you share a special connection to the other person. Perhaps you will select your soulmate, your twin flame, or your companion, spouse, close friend, or relative.
2. The downside to this approach is that you might feel too close to the person with whom you are sharing a lucid dream and focus unnecessarily on that companion as opposed to fully focusing on the lucid dream. The problem could start in the room where both of you recline, if you are unduly conscious of the other person in the room. The problem could continue at the dreamscape if you are preoccupied with your companion at the dream site. It is possible, of course, that you will not even observe each other at the dreamscape, since you will not be in your physical bodies but will appear only as energy bodies.
3. The setup for shared dreaming with a companion who starts with you in the same room is pretty much the same as the earlier exercise here. What you will need to begin and the procedure are basically the same. The only caution in preparation to leave the body is to tune out your companion and any observation of your companion when you tune out all exterior distractions. Then, when you arrive at the dreamscape and quickly orient yourself, you should totally ignore and block out any consciousness of your companion at the same site.
4. You will have time later, after your shared dream, to compare what you observed at the dreamscape and share any insights.

EXERCISE 5:
Joining a Group Dream

This is essentially similar to exercise 3 above. Instead of coordinating your dream with one other person as your dream companion, however, you will attempt to coordinate a group dream by agreeing with a group of people what and where you will program your lucid dream and what time you agree to embark on this shared dream. That is a classic programmed dream that is shared by a group of calculating friends who coordinate to dream together out of body.

It is also possible that you will randomly encounter a group of other dreamers during a lucid dream, since all of you could have a similar desire in visiting a certain time, place, and situation in a dreamscape. You might actually know some of these people. On the other hand, you might encounter them in a lucid-dream site only from time to time, with the off chance of possibly running into someone from your dreamscape during normal waking hours.

This is particularly true of the so-called *upper room*, where people gather in lucid dreams to learn from a master. You will frequently encounter a group of people—often the same people dream after dream, in these common learning situations. You will typically find yourself assembled in a grand room squatting in a circle, while a teacher comes out to address each one of you simultaneously. Since the teaching appears to be telepathic, there is no easy way to tell whether each and every member of your assembly is hearing the same message at the same time, although the master seems to address everyone at once in a way that is nonetheless personal.

Again, as in the previous exercise, try to tune out your dream companions throughout all phases of the shared lucid dream or allow them to pose a distraction. Focus solely on the dreamscape that unfolds before you as an insightful message of great personal importance to you on a deep level.

CHAPTER 20

Tips and Course Correction

Do not become discouraged if you find that you are not immediately able to set up and execute a perfect lucid dream outside space and time. Be patient, practice, and trust your inner self to lead the way. Totally shutting down the physical body and mind is alien to most people, who seem to fear doing so initially. There is nothing to fear. Your inner spirit will be in charge and care for you during a period of perfect rest and tranquility for your sleeping body.

The idea of drawing or painting pictures of what and where we want to go in a lucid dream is also alien to most of us, since our physical mind has unfortunately convinced most of us how words, sounds, and thoughts must flow endlessly through our heads. The mind, then, can become a gatekeeper that will not allow the superconsciousness of our inner self to come forward. Rather than slay the mind, try to subdue it to achieve harmony within your whole being. This will allow your spirit to rise. Your physical mind must be convinced that this is safe and within its best interest. It should eventually come to consider this occasion as a chance for a little rest and downtime during your lucid dream.

Do not concentrate to make any of this happen, since concentration is a function of the analytical mind that needs to shut down briefly. Instead, relax and reach a point of quiet stillness deep within you.

If you fail to proceed to reach any stage in setting up a lucid dream, then return to the starting point to try again. You can always try again. Practice is good for achieving success. You might find, for instance, that you cannot achieve full and proper physical rest or achieve conscious awareness. Or maybe you are unable to focus your intent upon the blank board to begin your creative visualization. Maybe you get stuck when it comes to you actually leaving the physical body and overcoming time and space. You might get that far but find it difficult to establish proper orientation at a dreamscape. Just go back to the beginning and restart the process.

(It is absolutely essential that you successfully transfer from physical brain analysis to heightened inner consciousness and fully accept the transfer without fear or reservation. This can be a sticking point for many people, who might move forward in setting up a lucid dream without reaching this harmony between the physical brain, which should be put asleep, and the superconsciousness, which should be allowed to direct activities after the physical brain is put to rest during the lucid-dream process. Fear of moving forward in proceeding with a lucid dream and leaving the body to roam during the dream will represent a failure to reach the inner harmony between body and spirit whereby inner consciousness takes charge.)

It is not enough to simply conceive of the dream. You must also be able to achieve and believe. That is the way that creative visualization works. It is three-part magic, and all three parts are important and necessary. Simply because you cannot see, hear, touch, taste, or smell something does not mean it is not ever present and waiting to be recognized. You are venturing into the hidden truths of the unseen world. The insights that you can gain in such a world in a self-directed lucid dream are enormous. They will enable your inner self to evolve. This is the most important part of you to develop on your long journey of discovery, since it will be with you forever.

Afterword

This book bears only slight resemblance to other dream books that you might have read. It differs from other books about lucid dreams in its approach, precautions, and realization that your lucid dreams when properly preprogrammed can take you anywhere in space-time or even outside the recognized world in which we physically live.

It is based on higher yoga and samadhi mysticism, so it requires an altered state of consciousness and focused intent. It requires you to think in pictures rather than words. It seeks a harmonic balance within your whole being to allow the physical mind to totally shut down so that the superconsciousness of your inner self—the eternal part of you—can emerge to explore outside normal space-time.

You may find that parts of this guidebook appear repetitive, but basic points in the process of programming your own lucid dream are so alien to our typical life that they need to be pounded deep within us to internalize the message. Consequently, this book follows the classic form of informational writing by telling you what we will discuss, then telling you, and then recapping what we have told you.

The overall approach in self-programming a lucid dream might seem alien to you, but it should not prove difficult if you carefully follow the steps. Even if you advance only partway through setting up a lucid dream and find that you need to start over, you still will have gained much by the initial steps you have achieved. Each step in itself, then, represents a significant improvement. Together, they can take you to uncharted journeys of discovery in a self-directed lucid dream.

Bibliography

Albert, Richard (Ram Das). *Be Here Now*. New York: Crown, 1971.

Anastopoulos, Charis. *Particle or Wave: The Evolution of the Concept of Matter in Modern Physics*. Princeton, NJ: Princeton University Press, 2008.

Arkani-Hamed, Nima, Savas Dimopoulous, and Georgi Dvali. "The Universe's Unseen Dimensions." *Scientific American* 283, no. 2 (August 2000): 62–69.

Arntz, William, Betty Chasse, and Mark Vicente. *What the Bleep Do We Know?* DVD. Los Angeles: 20th Century Fox, 2005.

Aurobindo, Sri. *The Secret of the Veda*. Pondicherry, India: Sri Aurobindo Ashram Publication, 1971.

Backster, Cleve. *Primary Perception: Biocommunication with Plants, Living Foods, and Human Cells*. Anza, CA: White Rose Millennium, 2003.

Bailey, Alice. *The Light of the Soul*. New York: Lucis, 1955.

Bailey, Alice, *A Treatise on White Magic*. New York: Lucis, 1998.

Barbour, Julian. *The End of Time: The Next Revolution in Physics*. New York: Oxford University Press, 2001.

Bartusiak, Marcia. *Einstein's Unfinished Symphony: Listening to the Sounds of Space-Time*. New York: Berkley Books, 2003.

Baum, L. Frank, and W. W. Denslow. *The Wonderful Wizard of Oz: The Original 1900 Edition in Full Color*. Independently published, 2021.

Bell, Madison Smartt. *Lavoisier in the Year One: The Birth of a New Science in an Age of Revolution*. New York: W. W. Norton, 2006.

Bentov, Itzhak. *Stalking the Wild Pendulum: On the Mechanics of Consciousness*. Rochester, VT: Destiny Books, 1998.

Besant, Annie. *The Bhagavad Gita: The Lord's Song*. Adyar, India: Theosophical Publishing House, 1953.

Besant, Annie. *Thought Power: In Control and Culture*. Wheaton, IL: Quest Books, 1967.

Besant, Annie, and Charles W. Leadbeater. *Thought-Forms*. Adyar, India: Theosophical Publishing Society, 1901.

Blavatsky, Helena P. *Collected Writings*. Adyar, India: Theosophical Publishing House, 1961.

Blavatsky Helena P. *The Secret Doctrine*. Adyar, India: Theosophical Society, 1986.

Blavatsky, Helena P. *The Voice of the Silence: Chosen Fragments from the Book of the Golden Precepts*. Chicago: Theosophy, 1928.

Bowman, Carol. *Children's Past Lives: How Past Memories Affect Your Child*. New York: Bantam, 1998.

Bradshaw, John. *Homecoming: Reclaiming and Championing Your Inner Child*. New York: Bantam, 1992.

Braschler, Von. *Ancient Wisdom Scrolls, Lucid Dreams*. Atglen, PA: REDFeather, 2022.
Braschler, Von. *Confessions of a Reluctant Ghost Hunter*. Rochester, VT: Destiny Books, 2014.
Braschler, Von. *Manifesting*. Atglen, PA: REDFeather, 2021.
Braschler, Von. *Mysterious Messages from Beyond*. Atglen, PA: REDFeather, 2021.
Braschler, Von. *Seven Secrets of Time Travel*. Rochester, VT: Destiny Books, 2012.
Braschler, Von. *Time Shifts*. Rochester, VT: Destiny Books, 2021.
Bryant, Edwin F. *The Yoga Sutras of Patanjali*. New York: North Point, 2009.
Castaneda, Carlos. *Journey to Ixtland*. New York: Washington Square, 1991.
Castaneda, Carlos. *A Separate Reality*. New York: Pocket Books, 1991.
Chao Kok Sui. *The Ancient Science & Art of Pranic Healing*. Quezon City, Philippines: Institute for Inner Studies, 1987.
Dash, Mike. "When Three British Boys Traveled to Medieval England (or Did They?)." *Smithsonian*, July 21, 2011.
Devi, Parama Karuna. *Bhagavata Purana*. CreateSpace, 2017.
Dossey, Larry. *Healing Words: The Power of Prayer and the Practice of Medicine*. New York: HarperCollins, 1993.
Dushkova, Zinovia. *The Secret Book of Dzyan: Unveiling the Hidden Truth about the Oldest Manuscript in the World and Its Divine Authors*. Moscow: Radiant Books, 2018.
Einstein, Albert. *The Theory of Relativity & Other Essays*. New York: MJF Books, 1955.
Emoto, Massaro. *The Hidden Messages in Water*. New York: Atria Books, 2005.
Emoto, Massaro. *Messages from Water and the Universe*. Carlsbad, CA: Hay House, 2010.
Emoto, Massaro. *The Miracle of Water*. New York: Atria Books, 2007.
Finney, Jack. "I'm Scared." *Collier's Magazine*, September 15, 1951.
Freud, Sigmund. *On Dreams*. New York: Dover, 2001.
Gawain, Shakti. *Creative Visualization*. Novato, CA: New World Library, 1978.
Gittner, Louis. *Listen, Listen, Listen*. Eastsound, WA: Louis Foundation, 1980.
Gittner, Louis. *Love Is a Verb*. Eastsound, WA: Touch the Heart, 1987.
Gittner, Louis. *There Is a Rainbow*. Eastsound, WA: Touch the Heart, 1981.
Goet, J. Richard. *Time Travel in Einstein's Universe: The Physical Possibilities of Travel through Time*. New York: Mariner Books, 2002.
Godwin, Joscelyn. *Harmonies of Heaven and Earth: The Spiritual Dimensions of Music*. Rochester, VT: Inner Traditions, 1987.
Hay, Louis. *Heal Your Body*. Carlsbad, CA: Hay House, 1988.
Heline, Corinne. *The Esoteric Music of Richard Wagner*. La Canada, CA: New Age, 1974.
Hirshfield, Alan. *The Electric Life of Michael Faraday*. New York: Walker, 2006.
Hobson, Allan. *Dream Consciousness*. New York: Spring, 2014.
Holy Bible, King James Version. Montgomery, IL: Christian Arts Publishers, 2013.
Hodson, Geoffrey. *Basic Theosophy*. Wheaton, IL: Quest Books, 1981.
Hodson, Geoffrey. *A Call to the Heights*. Wheaton, IL: Quest Books, 1975.
Homer. *The Iliad*. Translated by Robert Fagles. London: Penguin Classics, 1998.
Homer. *The Odyssey*. Translated by Robert Fagles. London: Penguin Classics, 1999.
Joseph, Frank. *Synchronicity & You: Understand the Role of Meaningful Coincidence in Your Life*. Rockport, MA: Element Books, 1999.
Joseph, Frank. *Synchronicity as Mystical Experience: Applying Meaning Coincidence in Your Life*. Pine Mountain Club, CA: Ancient Mysteries, 2018.
Jourdain, Eleanor, and Charlotte Moberly. *An Adventure*. Independently published, 2016.

Karagulla, Shafica, and Dora Van Gelder Kunz. *The Chakras and the Human Energy Fields.* Wheaton, IL: Theosophical Publishing House, 1998.
King, Serge Kahili. *Imagineering for Health.* Volcano, HI: Hunaworks, 2006.
Klemp, Harold. *The Dream Master.* Chanhassen, MN: Eckankar, 1997.
Krishnamurti, Jiddu. *At the Feet of the Master.* lulu.com, 2018.
Krishnamurti, Jiddu. *Commentaries on Living.* Wheaton, IL: Theosophical Publishing House, 1995.
Leadbeater, Charles W. *The Chakras.* Wheaton, IL: Theosophical Publishing House, 1997.
Leadbeater, Charles W. *Telepathy: The "Respectable" Phenomenon.* New York: Macmillan, 1971.
Leek, Sybil. *Diary of a Witch.* New York: Prentice Hall, 1968.
Lingerman, Hal. *The Healing Energies of Music.* Wheaton, IL: Theosophical Publishing House, 1995.
MacIsaac, Tara. "Accounts of People Who Seem to Literally Be from Parallel Universes." *Epoch Times*, May 6, 2016.
Maharishi Mahesh Yogi. *Science of Being and the Art of Living: Transcendental Meditation.* New York: Plume, 2001 (reissue).
Massey, Gerald. *The Natural Genesis.* Baltimore: Black Classic, 1998.
McKenzie, Andrew. *Adventures in Time: Encounters with the Past.* London: Athlone, 1997.
McLuhan, Marshall, and Quentin Fiore. *The Medium Is the Message.* New York: Random House, 1967.
Merleau-Ponty, Maurice. *Phenomenology of Perception.* Translated by Colin Smith. London: Rutledge & Kegan, 1962.
Milton, John. *Paradise Lost.* New York: Penguin Classics 2003.
Murphet, Howard. *Sai Baba: Man of Miracles.* York Beach, ME: Red Wheel / Weiser, 1977.
Montgomery, S. R. *The Second Law of Thermodynamics.* Oxford: Pergamon, 1966.
Nagy, Andras M. *The Secrets of Pythagoras.* Charleston, SC: CreateSpace, 2007.
Narby, Jeremy. *Intelligence in Nature: An Inquiry into Knowledge.* New York: Jeremy Tarcher, 2005.
Newton, Michael. *Journey of Souls.* St. Paul, MN: Llewellyn, 1999.
Olcott, Henry Steele. *Old Diary Leaves.* Wheaton, IL: Theosophical Publishing House, 1975.
Ostrander, Sheila, Lynn Shroeder, and Ivan T. Sanderson. *Psychic Discoveries behind the Iron Curtain.* New York: Bantam Books, 1971.
Ouspensky, P. D. *A New Model of the Universe.* New York: Dover, 1997.
Ouspensky, P. D. *In Search of the Miraculous.* Boston: Mariner Books, 2001.
Ouspensky, P. D. *Tertium Origanum.* Kila, MT: Kessinger, 1998.
Paulson, Genevieve Lewis. *Energy Focused Meditation.* St. Paul, MN: Llewellyn, 1997.
Perls, Frederick, Ralph Hefferline, and Paul Goodman. *Gestalt Therapy.* London: Souvenir, 1995.
Pierrakos, John. *Core Energetics.* Mendocino, CA: Evolution, 2005.
Plato. *Complete Words by Plato.* Indianapolis, IN: Hackett, 1997.
Puharich, Andreija. *Uri: The Original and Authorized Biography of Uri Geller, the Man Who Baffled Scientists.* London: W. H. Allen, 1974.
Radha, Swami Sivananda. *Light & Vibration: Consciousness, Mysticism & the Culmination of Yoga.* Kootenay Bay, BC: Timeless Books, 2007.
Richards, Steve. *Invisibility: Mastering the Art of Vanishing.* London: Thorsons, 1992.
Ritkin, Jeremy. *Entropy: Into the Greenhouse World.* New York: Bantam Books, 1989.

Roberts, Jane. *Seth Speaks: The Eternal Validity of the Soul*. Novato, CA: New World Library, 1994.
Salazar, Michael. *The Witch and the Spymaster: World Ward 2 in Europe*. Amazon Digital Services, 2014.
Satchedananda, Sri S. *The Yoga Sutras of Pantanjali*. Buckingham, VA: Integral Yoga Distribution, 1990.
Sedgwick, Icy. "Time Slips: Urban Legend, Ghost Story, or Utter Nonsense?" www.icysedgwick.com/time-slips. September 14, 2019.
Skolimowski. Henryk. *Theatre of the Mind*. Wheaton, IL: Quest Books, 1984.
Smith, Ingram. *Truth Is a Pathless Land: A Journey with Krishnamurti*. Wheaton, IL: Quest Books, 1989.
Smith, Penelope. *Animals… Our Return to Wholeness*. Point Reyes Station, CA: Pegasus, 1993.
Snowden, Ruth. *The Key Ideas from Analytical Psychology and Dreams to the Collective Unconsciousness and More*. London: Teach Yourself Books, 2017.
Steiger, Brad. *One with the Light: Authentic Near-Death Experience That Changed Lives and Revealed the Beyond*. New York: Signet, 1994.
Steiger. Brad. *Words from the Source*. Englewood Cliffs, NJ: Prentice-Hall, 1975.
Steriade, Mircea, and Robert McCarley. *Brain Control of Wakefulness and Sleep*. New York: Springer, 2015.
Stevenson, Ian. *Children Who Remember Previous Lives*. Jefferson, NC: McFarland, 2000.
Stone, Robert B. *The Secret Life of Your Cells*. Atglen: PA. Schiffer, 1997.
Strager, Hanne, and Sarah Darwin. *A Modest Genius: The Story of Darwin's Life and How His Ideas Changed Everything*. CreateSpace, 2016.
Tarnow, Eugen. *Serial Position Curve of Free Recall Repeats*. Amazon, 2018.
Tarnow, Eugen, and Regina Erchova. *Working Memory Capacities Differ by Academic Field*s: Sports Teachers on Top. Kindle edition, independently published, 2018.
Telang, Vensa, and Kashinath Trimbak Telang. *The Bhagavad Gita*. Digireads.com, 2017.
Tiller, William A., Walter Dibble, and Michael Kohane. *Conscious Acts of Creation*. Walnut Creek, CA: Pavior, 2001
Tompkins, Peter. *Secrets of the Soil*. Anchorage, AK: Earthpulse, 1989.
Tompkins, Peter, and Christopher Bird. *The Secret Life of Plants*. New York: Harper & Row, 1989.
Twitchell, Paul. *The Tiger's Fang*. Menlo Park, CA: Illuminated Way, 1967.
Vance, Bruce A. *Dreamscape: Voyage in an Alternate Reality*. Wheaton, IL: Quest Books, 1995.
Vance, Bruce. *Mindscape: Exploring the Reality of Thought Forms*. Wheaton, IL: Quest Books, 1995.
Wagner, Stephen. "Time Travelers: Journeys into the Past and Future." LiveAbout, https//weirddarkness.com.time-travel-true-stories, PDFCoffee. August 14, 2018.
Webster, Richard. *Aura Reading for Beginners*. St. Paul, MN: Llewellyn, 1998.
Weschcke, Carl, and Joe Slate. *Self-Empowerment and the Subconscious*. Woodbury, MN: Llewellyn, 2018.
Wood, Ernest. *The Seven Rays*. Wheaton, IL: Theosophical Publishing House, 1972.

Index

A

accomplishment, 39, 61
acute, 17, 30, 31, 32, 34, 42, 45, 50, 62, 64, 71, 73, 75, 76, 78, 87, 96, 102, 103, 104, 105, 110, 115, 120, 127, 141, 146
adventure, 16, 19, 34, 45, 47, 51, 58, 59, 66, 69, 80, 82, 86, 88, 90, 99, 100, 101, 102, 103, 105, 112, 118, 128, 131, 132,141, 142
agenda, 21, 44, 66, 69, 77, 78, 80, 81, 82, 84, 85, 91, 105, 110, 112, 115, 117, 118, 121, 123, 127, 135, 137, 138, 141, 142, 146
altered state, 9, 27, 57, 60, 66, 80, 89, 90, 91, 94, 139
alternate reality, 16, 120, 125
analysis, 29, 36, 37, 43, 45, 64, 71, 73, 74, 76, 78, 79, 89, 99, 107, 108, 110, 111, 116, 137, 142, 146, 150
analyze, 2, 3, 4, 9, 37, 40, 43, 70, 71, 74, 75, 76, 79, 100, 101, 107, 108, 109, 110, 111, 116, 128, 135, 137, 139, 142, 146
Arjuna, 44, 57, 118
artists, 27
Assyrians, 23
awareness, 10, 17, 18, 19, 30, 31, 32, 33, 34, 36, 40, 42, 45, 52, 56, 60, 62, 64, 71, 73, 75, 78, 84, 86, 87, 91, 95, 96, 97, 98, 99, 102, 103, 104, 105, 110, 115, 120, 121, 127, 129, 133, 134, 139, 141, 145, 146, 149

B

Babylonia, 1, 23
Bailey, Alice,152
baseball, 54, 106
Besant, Annie, 124, 152
Bible, 61, 63, 64
Blavatsky, Helena, 88, 152
brain, 5, 13, 14, 15, 16, 17, 18, 28, 29, 30, 33, 36, 37, 38, 39, 40, 41, 43, 47, 48, 50, 53, 54, 55, 58, 86, 94, 108, 110, 133, 134, 135, 150
Buddhism, 25, 26

C

Castaneda, Carlos, 31, 62
causal body, 21, 32, 42, 65, 71, 73, 75, 78, 96, 127, 128
chakras, 9, 154
Christianity, 25, 26
clear, 18, 70, 75, 77, 80, 95, 110, 127, 143
color, 14, 21, 30, 31, 44, 50, 65, 83, 88, 102, 115
common dreams, 13, 14, 28, 29, 30, 35, 36, 39, 40, 41, 45, 108, 112
concerns, 12, 13, 15, 29, 37, 38, 39, 40, 41, 51, 57, 58, 66, 67, 68, 81, 86, 94, 95, 97, 108, 109, 126, 131, 137
confidence, 28, 65, 66, 67, 82, 113, 121, 137, 138, 143
connotative meaning, 42
cosmos, cosmic, 44, 45, 63, 123
course correction, 11, 12, 149
creative, 9, 11, 32, 54, 61, 65, 66, 67, 69, 117, 126, 129, 131, 139, 143, 149, 150

D

dense, 31, 41, 53, 68, 83, 103, 127
destination, 6, 11, 44, 80, 82, 92, 99, 102, 122, 124, 146
dimensions, 7, 89, 119, 120, 129, 139, 141
discovery, 9, 10, 11, 12, 14, 17, 19, 23, 30, 31, 32, 34, 41, 42, 44, 45, 46, 47, 49, 51, 52, 57, 64, 65, 68, 69, 72, 79, 80, 81, 82, 84, 86, 89, 94, 99, 100,101, 103, 105, 106, 108, 109, 110, 112, 118, 124, 128, 131, 133, 141, 150
divine, 14, 23, 24, 25, 26, 39, 41, 44, 57, 63
Dorothy (from the *Wizard of Oz*), 46, 100, 102, 106, 118
dreamscape, 11, 12, 16, 18, 28, 30, 31, 34, 41, 42, 44, 47, 48, 49, 50, 51, 64, 65, 66, 68, 69, 70, 71, 72, 73, 74, 75, 76, 77, 78, 80, 81, 82, 84, 85, 86, 87, 91, 94, 96, 97, 98, 99, 100, 102, 103, 104, 105, 106, 110, 111,112, 113, 115, 116, 117, 118, 125,

Index

126, 127, 128, 129, 130, 133, 135, 136, 137, 138, 141, 142, 144, 145, 146, 148, 148, 150
dreamwork, 9, 39, 41, 46, 66, 82, 91, 102, 106, 107, 108, 112, 119, 125, 144

E
Egyptians, 9, 23, 24
electromagnetic, 30, 35, 38, 49, 68, 83, 91, 98, 113, 125
energy, 19, 21, 29, 30, 31, 32, 34, 35, 38, 44, 47, 49, 50, 53, 54, 56, 58, 59, 64, 65, 66, 68, 70, 71, 72, 73, 75, 77, 78, 83, 86, 92, 95, 96, 97, 113, 114, 119, 122, 124, 125, 127, 128, 129, 130, 137, 140, 141, 142, 143, 144, 145
energy body, 10, 21, 32, 44, 49, 89, 95, 96, 97, 119, 127, 128, 129, 133, 141, 146
eternal, 11, 41, 42, 52, 64, 66, 81, 88, 91, 113, 117, 119, 121, 123, 125, 132, 138, 151
evolution, 38, 52, 99, 106, 118
exercises, 70, 72, 74, 77, 140, 142, 144, 147
expectation, 40, 45, 60

F
fire within, 42, 52
flame, 19, 20, 41, 42, 43, 116, 117, 119, 147
focus, 10, 11, 13, 19, 20, 21, 28, 29, 31, 32, 33, 34, 40, 43, 45, 47, 48, 49, 50, 51, 58, 60, 61, 62, 64, 65, 66, 67, 71, 72, 73, 75, 76, 77, 78, 87, 91, 95, 96, 97, 101, 102, 104, 108, 109, 110, 112, 114, 115, 116, 117, 120, 121, 122, 124, 126, 127, 129, 131, 132, 133, 134, 139, 140, 141, 142, 143, 145, 146, 147, 148, 149, 151
Freud, Sigmund, 5, 7, 37, 38
future, 6, 7, 9, 10, 11, 13, 14, 18, 19, 21, 26, 42, 44, 45, 50, 63, 66, 83, 84, 86, 87, 88, 90, 91, 92, 93, 97, 98, 105, 108, 109, 115, 119, 121, 122, 125, 126
future lives, 7, 88, 98

G
game, 106
geometric, 42
Gilgamesh, 23
Gittner, Louis, 46, 153
gnosis, 42, 128
Greeks, 24
growth, 41, 102, 104, 122
guide, 6, 9, 10, 11, 12, 23, 25, 41, 49, 51, 56, 60, 63, 66, 67, 68, 69, 71, 73, 75, 76, 77, 78, 79, 80, 81, 82, 83, 84, 85, 96, 97, 101, 103, 106, 117, 139, 143, 144

H
harmony, 11, 48, 53, 57, 58, 59, 133, 134, 135, 136, 140, 143, 145, 149, 150
heal, healing, 5, 24, 31, 45
heavy, 47, 114, 124, 132, 140, 142, 145
hero, 57, 88, 12, 103
hero's journey, 11, 45, 51, 52, 69, 81, 99, 100, 101, 104, 105, 106
Hindu, 25, 44, 57, 60, 64
history, 6, 9, 24, 26, 91, 107, 108
Hobson, Allan, 38, 153
Hodson, Geoffrey, 153
Homer, 100, 105, 153
horse, 102, 115
hypnosis, 56, 109

I
impact, 14, 42, 45, 51, 52, 65, 83, 91, 108, 113, 116, 117, 124, 125, 126, 127, 129
implications, 86, 124, 125, 126, 129, 130, 131
Indigenous tribes, 25, 26
intent, 9, 10, 11, 20, 21, 23, 28, 30, 31, 32, 43, 45, 47, 48, 49, 50, 51, 52, 64, 65, 66, 67, 87, 91, 95, 96, 101, 102, 104, 105, 106, 108, 110, 115, 116, 117, 120, 121, 122, 124, 126, 131, 139, 141, 145, 149, 151
Islam, 13, 27, 46, 160

J
Jewish, 25
journal, 12, 30, 40, 43, 71, 74, 76, 79, 107, 108, 109, 110, 111, 122
journey, 6, 9, 10, 11, 12, 14, 18, 21, 26, 31, 32, 34, 41, 42, 44, 45, 47, 51, 52, 56, 66, 68, 69, 71, 72, 73, 74, 75, 76, 78, 80, 81, 82, 86, 88, 89, 90, 91, 92, 94, 95, 99, 100, 101, 102, 103, 104, 105, 106, 110, 112, 118, 119, 124, 132, 150, 151
Jung, Carl, 5, 7, 37, 118

K
Karagulla, Shafica, 154
karma, 7, 21, 43, 44, 50, 116, 118
Klemp, Harold, 67, 82, 154
Krishnamurti, Jiddu, 62, 64, 124, 134, 154
Kunz, Dora Van Gelder, 154

L
Leadbeater, Charles, 124, 152, 154
Leek, Sybil, 88, 154
light, 19, 20, 31, 38, 41, 46, 54, 57, 64, 70, 71, 72, 73, 74, 75, 77, 78, 83, 97, 96, 117, 122, 152, 155
linear thinking, 34

lucid, 5, 6, 7, 9, 10, 11, 12, 14, 15, 16, 17, 18, 19, 22, 23, 28, 30, 31, 32, 34, 35, 36, 38, 39, 40, 41, 42, 43, 44, 45, 46, 47
Luther, Martin, 28

M

magnet, 30, 35, 38, 49, 65, 68, 83, 91, 98, 113, 116, 122, 125, 143
map, 6, 10, 11, 20, 21, 32, 44, 45, 48, 49, 61, 64, 65, 66, 68, 69, 70, 71, 72, 73, 74, 75, 76, 77, 78, 79, 80, 81, 82, 84, 85, 87, 89, 90, 91, 93, 95, 96, 101, 103, 104, 105, 112, 113, 114, 115, 116, 117, 118, 121, 135, 136, 141, 145
material reductionists, 35
McCarley, Robert, 38, 155
medical, 35, 38, 53, 92
meditate, meditation, 10, 15, 17, 18, 21, 22, 40, 45, 48, 53, 54, 55, 56, 57, 60, 71, 74, 76, 79, 99, 109, 110,113, 115, 120, 128, 130, 133, 134, 135, 137, 139, 140, 142, 144, 147, 154
memories, 5, 11, 13, 14, 15, 17, 29, 30, 33, 34, 36, 37, 38, 39, 54, 71, 74, 76, 79, 86, 108, 110, 135,152
Mesopotamia, 23
mind, 5, 11, 13, 14, 15, 16, 17, 20, 21, 28, 29, 30, 31, 33, 34, 39, 40, 41, 43, 45, 48, 53, 54, 56, 57, 58, 59, 61, 66, 70, 72, 73, 74, 75, 76, 77, 78, 79, 80, 86, 94, 95, 98, 99, 102, 106, 108, 109, 110, 111, 126, 132, 133, 134, 136, 137, 139, 140, 143, 145, 149, 151
mind's eye, 20, 21, 44, 48, 49, 65, 66, 70, 73, 75, 78, 80, 81, 82, 84, 91, 93, 95, 114, 117, 120, 122, 123, 135, 136, 137, 139
movement, 14, 33, 35, 36, 38, 52, 55, 95, 126, 129
moving reality, 33, 67
multiverse, 89, 120

N

neurologists, neurological, 35, 38
new ears, 31, 61, 86, 97, 105, 126
new eyes, 18, 31, 50, 61, 64, 71, 73, 76, 78, 83, 86, 97, 105, 120, 126, 127, 129
Newton, Isaac, 119, 154

O

observer, 17, 97, 104, 124, 126, 127, 128,129, 136
Odysseus, 88, 100, 102, 106, 118
orienting, 50, 84, 96
Ouspensky, P. D., 88, 89, 120, 154

out of body, 43, 88, 99, 101, 122, 126, 128, 129, 134, 148

P

parallel reality, 16, 121, 122, 123, 124
parallel universe, 6, 88, 89, 154
parallel world, 120, 121, 122, 123, 124, 125
past, 5, 6, 7, 9, 10, 11, 13, 14, 18, 20, 21, 28, 33, 34, 38, 42, 45, 50, 63, 65, 81, 86, 87, 89, 90, 91, 92, 98, 102, 105, 108, 109, 121, 122, 125, 126
past lives, 90, 91, 121
perception, 31, 34, 48, 57, 59, 62, 71, 73, 76, 78, 90, 95, 110, 120, 121, 127, 140, 143, 145
Perls, 37, 154
physical body, 9, 11, 12, 15, 18, 19, 20, 21, 24, 26, 28, 29, 31, 32, 34, 39, 41, 42, 47, 48, 49, 50, 56, 58, 59, 61, 67, 68, 69, 70, 71, 72, 73, 74, 75, 76, 77, 78, 79, 81, 82, 84, 86, 87, 94, 95, 96, 97, 98, 99, 106, 108, 110, 113, 114, 124, 127, 128, 131, 132, 133, 134, 136, 137, 139, 140, 141,142, 143, 145, 146, 149
physical mind, 29, 30, 34, 48, 53, 56, 57, 58, 70, 71, 72, 74, 75, 76, 77, 79, 94, 99, 102, 106, 108, 111, 114, 127, 130, 131, 132, 133, 134, 135, 136, 137, 140, 142, 143, 145, 149, 151
Plato, 89, 154
preparation, 39, 46, 84, 95, 117, 147
program, 9, 10, 11, 12, 18, 19, 21, 22, 28, 29, 30, 32, 36, 38, 45, 47, 48, 53, 60, 69, 79, 97, 104, 106, 112, 115, 116, 117, 122, 124, 131, 138, 139, 141, 142, 144, 147
prophecy, 23, 24, 25
psychologists, 14, 105, 107, 108
pyramid, 42

R

raja-yoga, 10, 55, 60, 129
random, 5, 6, 14, 15, 36, 39, 40, 41, 42, 43, 45, 67, 90, 91, 109, 110, 119, 129, 149
rapid eye movement, 14, 35, 36, 38
reality, 10, 14, 16,17, 31, 33, 34, 37, 41, 46, 47, 51, 59, 61, 62, 64, 67, 82, 87, 88, 98, 120, 121, 122, 123, 125, 129, 136
realization, 39, 47, 99, 151
recall, 21, 28, 36, 48, 49, 51, 71, 73, 75, 76, 78, 95, 109, 114, 118, 136, 141, 142, 143, 145, 146, 155
recurring dreams, 5, 14, 37, 43, 109
reflect, reflection, 3, 14, 15, 17, 22, 26, 31, 34, 58, 64, 96, 110, 128, 134, 137

remote viewing, 87
restless dreams, 15, 17, 30, 49, 108, 109
restless mind, 13, 14, 28, 30, 31, 33, 34, 36, 40, 45, 48, 86, 108, 110
return, 11, 12, 15, 18, 21, 22, 25, 42, 45, 51, 52, 59, 67, 68, 71, 72, 73, 74, 76, 78, 79, 87, 92, 94, 97, 98, 99, 100, 101, 104, 105, 106, 109, 110, 132, 137, 138, 139, 142,146, 149
review, 28, 33, 34, 35, 39, 40, 66, 81, 108, 109, 110, 136, 137

S
safety, 53, 55, 58, 94, 101
Samadhi, 10, 26, 36, 55, 151
science, 31, 35, 36, 53, 57, 152, 153, 154
security, 11, 34, 55, 94, 98, 131
self-directed, 9, 10, 11, 22, 44, 45, 46, 51, 58, 59, 69, 80, 103, 104, 116, 122, 124, 129, 131, 139, 140, 144, 150
senses, 18, 34, 42, 55, 56, 61, 62, 63, 64, 86, 88, 96, 98, 109, 120, 133, 134
shamans, shamanism, 9, 10, 36, 56, 57, 61, 62, 97, 120, 125
shared dreams, 11, 112, 115, 139, 144
site, 21, 54, 125, 131, 136, 137, 141, 145, 146, 147, 148
slate, 43, 48, 66, 69, 70, 72, 73, 74, 75, 77, 78, 80, 81, 82, 84, 89, 91, 92, 93, 95, 114, 117, 120, 122, 123, 135, 136, 137, 138, 140, 141, 143, 145, 146
slay, 53, 57, 133, 149
sleep, 9, 11,13, 14, 16, 18, 19, 20, 21, 22, 23, 24, 26, 27, 28, 29, 30, 33, 34, 35, 36, 37, 38, 40, 47, 48, 49, 52, 56, 63, 68, 70, 71, 72, 74, 75, 76, 77, 79, 86, 94, 108, 109, 110, 114, 130, 131, 132, 134, 140, 141, 142, 143, 145, 149, 150
space, 9, 10, 14, 15, 16, 17, 19, 21, 26, 28, 29, 31, 32, 34, 43, 44, 45, 48, 49, 56, 57, 60, 66, 68, 69, 70, 71, 73, 79, 80, 82, 86, 87, 89, 93, 94, 96, 97, 101, 102,103, 104, 106, 118, 119, 122, 123, 129, 132, 133, 136, 139, 141, 142, 149, 151, 152
space-time, 9, 17, 86, 97, 151, 152
spark, 4
spirit, 9, 10, 11,14, 18, 26, 27, 31, 32, 34, 38, 39, 41, 42, 43, 44, 48, 49, 50, 52, 53, 54, 55, 56, 57, 58, 59, 61, 62, 63, 64, 65, 66, 68, 69, 72, 73, 74, 79, 80, 81, 82, 84, 85, 86, 87, 88, 89, 91, 93, 94, 95, 96, 100, 101, 103, 104, 110, 111, 112,113, 114, 115, 118, 119, 120, 121, 122, 123, 128, 129, 130, 137, 138, 141, 149, 150

subconscious, 5, 15, 17, 37, 38, 40, 134, 156
subtle body, 71, 73, 76, 78
Sumer, 23
superconsciousness, 35, 38, 134, 135, 149, 150
superficial, 13, 31, 32, 38, 44, 48, 54, 59, 60, 81

T
tablet, 75, 141, 143
Tarnow, Eugen, 36, 37, 155
temples, 9, 24, 108
theatre, 33, 155
theosophy, theosophical, 152, 153, 154
thought forms, 66, 67, 113, 114, 116, 122, 124, 126, 143, 155
thought power, 66, 87, 113, 152
three-stage magical formula, 46
time, 6, 7, 10, 11, 15, 16, 18, 19, 21, 26, 32, 36, 44, 45, 56, 60, 65, 66, 84, 86, 90, 91, 92, 93, 95, 96, 97, 103, 112, 113, 114, 115, 118, 121, 122, 123, 125, 132, 133, 136, 141, 152
tips, 12, 149
triangle, 42
Twitchell, Paul, 155

V
Vance, Bruce, 18, 31, 155
vibration, 65, 135, 155
visiting, 21, 25, 90, 97, 106, 114, 118, 122, 123, 124, 128, 148
visualization, 11, 60, 61, 65, 66, 67, 69, 103, 116, 117, 126,129, 131, 149, 150, 153
vivid, 9, 14, 16, 18, 23, 24, 26, 28, 30, 31, 32, 33, 39, 41, 43, 49, 67, 79, 84, 103, 105, 118, 122, 131, 137, 139

W
Welsh, 24
wholeness, 45, 51, 57, 58, 59, 61, 81, 100, 101, 106, 135, 155
will, 65, 71, 73, 103
wisdom yoga, 10, 60
witness, 18, 32, 33, 44, 71, 73, 76, 78, 84, 91, 97, 104, 121, 126, 128, 137, 141, 146

Y
yoga, 10, 26, 47, 53, 55, 57, 60, 120, 129, 133, 151
yoga masters, 10, 120
Yoga Sutras, 153, 155

About the Author

Von Braschler is the author of many books on consciousness development, dreams, energy healing, and time, including *Manifesting* and *Mysterious Messages from Beyond*.

He has lectured and led workshops through the United States and the United Kingdom and served as a faculty member at Omega Institute for Holistic Studies in New York. Braschler has appeared on many radio and television programs. He was a host of a popular podcast called *Healing with Your Pet: Our Psychic, Spiritual Connection* for four years. Previously he worked as an award-winning journalist and publisher of his own community newspaper in Alaska and regional magazine in Washington State. He lives and writes on a rustic, little island in the San Juans near Anacortes, Washington. Visit him on Facebook @vbraschler and www.vonbraschlerwebsite.com.